Conquering Uncertainty

Conquering Uncertainty

Don't concede too soon, your Victory awaits you

TAMEKA C. MCNAIR

TABLE OF CONTENTS

ACKNOWLEDGMENTS

Thank you to my mother who chose to 'keep me' during one of the many moments of uncertainty that she has endured, through her sacrifice I have a story to tell.

Thank you to my father (rest in heaven) who gave me the gift of a 'sincere apology' for his absence in my upbringing, healing a major area in my heart.

Thank you to my "Fav 7": Monica (Pooh), Evan, Laura, Lucy, Amanda, Denise and Samaj who contributed to my writing process in such a meaning way! You each played a vital part in taking this book from a concept to bringing it to reality. Your sacrifice of time and generosity of spirit is greatly appreciated. I love you dearly!!!

Special acknowledgment to My Baby Loves (twin boys) - October 2006 changed my life forever. I never experienced the True Magnitude of LOVE until I gave birth to you two. You are the best parts of me.

PREFACE

Recently, I realized that I don't give myself as much credit as I deserve. When I share my story of utter devastation, the heart break's that showed me my worth and breaking free from imposter syndrome — the consistent response that I get is "Wow, how did you do that? I can't even imagine having to deal with a fraction of what you've been through." One of the mottos that I live by is to reach for the stars and do not stop until you obtain them all. I acknowledge the challenges along the journey but don't let them stop my forward movement.

As I reflect on my experiences, there is a consistent theme: my ability to thrive in the midst of uncertainty. In this book, you'll find vulnerable examples of times of uncertainty in my life and lessons that will give you the practical tools that you can use when encountering times of uncertainty in your own life. If I can thrive in the midst of all the moments of uncertainty, so can you.

Moments of uncertainty for me began when I was in my mother's womb. A 27-year-old woman with two small children finds out that she's pregnant by a man who she still loved a few weeks after their break-up. The timing couldn't have been any worse. In the middle of picking up the pieces of her broken heart, she had to process the fact that she was carrying his baby. Confused, conflicted, and caught up in a conundrum of emotions, she was left contemplating two options: keep this baby or have an abortion.

After consulting with people in her close circle, my mother made the decision to undergo an abortion, even receiving money from a mother figure to support this decision. The appointment was made, and the time confirmed. The decision appeared to be final. Moments before walking through the steel double doors of the clinic, an overwhelming conviction came over this single mother of two sons. "This could be the daughter that you always wanted. If you can take care of two, you can take care of three." I truly thank God for that gentle voice inside of her that kept her from aborting me. My mother carried me in her womb filled with so much uncertainty about what the future would hold, yet her decision is the very reason that I am able to share my story with you today.

We all have had moments of uncertainty in our lives, for me those moments started from the time of my mother's womb and continues to surface in every facet of my life. I am living my mission of "Empowering everyone that I encounter to become the best version of themselves and to discover purpose" through writing this book in hopes of inspiring each and every person who opens this book **to** *not concede too soon in moments of uncertainty, as your victory awaits you*. This is my journey of forgiveness, healing, self-actualization, perseverance, hope and unconditional love as I have navigated my moments of uncertainty. Free from shame as I own each part of my narrative, not letting anyone dictate my path forward because of my past. I encourage you to own your narrative without shame, pursue your audacious goals with tenacity, forgive yourself and others along the journey, and make a lasting impact on the world.

CONQUERING UNCERTAINTY is a 3-step process to self - actualization. You will learn to:

1) Own your own destiny: Don't let anyone talk you out of what you want because you are afraid. Don't think that you do not deserve what you want or fear that because you've never seen it before, you cannot achieve it.

Of the guiding principles that have helped me navigate the seven stories shared in the book, embracing **Positivity** is the common guiding principle.

❖ **My Guiding Principles:**
Faith, Perseverance, Focus, Agility, Determination, Identity, Confidence, Forgiveness, Peace, Purpose-Driven, Sacrifice, Compassion, Love, Intentionality and Positivity.

2) Stick to your dreams and passions

How do you continue to add wood to the fire and stay true to yourself? Don't buy into the narrative that others write for you. Stick to your own narrative and do the work to make it real. Believe in yourself.

Your authentic self is the greatest gift to yourself and the world. There is liberation when you dare to be the person you naturally are. Actualization and determination at the same time (found a way to push through obstacles).

❖ When I have stayed true to myself, I have had the greatest peace, made the greatest decisions.

3) Thrive in the space you are in now

Other people's affirmations are unnecessary. Validation must come from within. The decisions that I made at each moment of uncertainty brought me to the place of thriving.

Fulfill your life purpose: Do you know the impact that you are meant to make on the world? I am fulfilling my life purpose of helping others, walking in love, inspiring others to become the best version of themselves through writing this book.

❖ Set audacious goals and commit to making a positive impact to the lives of others around you.

At the end of each chapter, there is a reflection exercise where you will have an opportunity to put the lessons that I share into practice.

CHAPTER ONE
DEVASTATION:
I THOUGHT I WOULD LOSE MY MIND

It was early in the morning on November 19th, 2006. This day appeared to be no different than the prior 34 days since my twin boys entered the world, but it was to unfold in a way I could not have prepared myself for.

My sons were born six weeks earlier than expected and received them with immense anticipation and excitement. These two beautiful boys changed my life the moment I heard their cries. As the doctors placed one son at a time briefly on my chest before taking them to the scale and weighing their tiny bodies, I heard "Baby A, 6 lbs. 2 oz... Baby B 6 lbs. and 4 oz." I drifted in and out of sleep due to the medication that was placed in my IV prior to the C-section.

The next thing I remember is waking up in my hospital room where we would be occupants for the next 3-4 days. My eyes barely open as slight aches ran up and down my body, I asked "Where are my babies?" After calling for a nurse, two promptly entered the room asking, "How can I assist you?"

"I'm ready to see my babies."

One nurse responded with a mild shaky tone in her voice, "One of your babies is in the ICU. He swallowed meconium microrems while he was in the womb. We have to monitor him until he's in a more stable place. Although we can't bring him to your room, we can wheel you over there when you are ready. In the meantime, we're bringing baby 'A' to your room."

In the moment, all I could think about was the well-being of my baby 'B.' This precious gift that at this point I only had one opportunity to hear his little voice from his first cry.

The door squeaked lightly as they returned with Baby A in his incubator sleeping like an angel. Full head of black hair with a slightly curl pattern across his tiny little head. My heart instantly melted; it was love at first sight. My nurse swooped the baby up with a gentle touch and placed him on my chest for our first skin-to-skin contact encounter.

Those who are mothers know that the skin-to-skin contact encounter is the most important and intimate step in bonding with your newborn child. I cannot even put into words the feeling that I felt the moment this tiny little baby's skin connected with my own. Truly a euphoric moment. I'm positive it compares to the moment that a climber arrives at the peak of mount Everest! Moving like a little snail for a brief moment until he found his comfortable spot, then shifting into his angelic state of rest.

As my baby laid on my chest there were a million thoughts that went through my head.

"This is real, the babies who spent the last 36 weeks in my belly have finally arrived."

"Am I ready for this?"

"Will I measure up and be the mother that they need me to be?"

"Is it possible to still finish my college degree in engineering?"

"Who will they grow up and become?"

"Will they be independent and have a voice that they are not afraid to use?"

"How will I manage raising two babies and still maintain my schoolwork?"

The questions went on –and on, as I wondered about my future and theirs. I became so lost in thoughts that I nearly missed the moment of bonding with my precious newborn.

As I looked down at his perfectly shaped little head, the smile in my heart matched that on my face. I was able to have this incredibly special moment with one of my baby boys, but I felt incomplete with Baby B placed in an incubator in an isolated room. This special moment was supposed to be with both of my babies who shared my womb together.

I called for the nurse and asked for the status of my other baby boy and when I would be able to see him. She responded, "He's in stable condition. We had to give him some oxygen and we're monitoring him to make sure his body is functioning appropriately. His skin tone has a slight yellow tint so we're also monitoring him for jaundice. Once you're ready to get out of bed, we'll take you down to see him. Since he's in the ICU unit, you won't be able to hold him but will be able to see him through the glass incubator." Wheeled down the long hallway clothed in my hospital rope with a thin white blanket covering my legs, while baby 'A' slept like an angel in the crib placed to the right of my bed.

As I pushed my face as close as I could to the incubator without making direct contact, the first thing that I noticed was his head full of black straight hair and the extra fingers that were on both of his hands just like his baby brother. Having an extra finger on your hands is very common for the men in my family; however, it is rare for duo siblings in a direct family to have them. Out of my mother's eight siblings, only one of them has an extra finger.

I proceeded with a scan over my baby as if my eyes were x-ray radars, paying detailed attention to everything that was visible to the eye. His fair skin tone appeared to be as soft as a piece of silk fabric with the perfect little hands and toes, nothing seemed to be out of place about him not even one stray hair out of position. I got lost in the moment admiring this beautiful baby, wishing I could home him against my chest.

In the middle of this feeling of greatness, a wave of sadness washed over me like waves over the deep blue sea. The reality that I could not hold my baby in my arms and feel his heart connect with mine, that I could not share the moment with my twins together, was overwhelming. I kept these feelings to myself because I was concerned about how I would be perceived if anyone knew the inner turmoil that I was battling. Misplaced guilt about the boys not sharing their first moments with each other outside of my womb, which they had spent the last 34 weeks together. Thinking that I had something to this unforeseeable circumstance, I couldn't help but place the blame on myself for my baby swallowing meconium.

Thoughts raced through my head:

"Maybe you're not cut out for this."

"You have no clue what you are doing!"

"What mother doesn't get to hold her newborn after giving birth?"

"Maybe what you ate before you went into labor is what caused this."

These three days of my baby being in the NICU, apart from me and his brother, felt like an eternity. *Is he going to be, okay? How many days will he have to stay in an isolated room? Will he be able to head home with us when I'm released from the hospital?*

Mostly questions, no answers.

My stay at the hospital was a little longer than normal

because of the C-section. As I sat up in my bed worrying about going home on my release date, it felt as if I were sitting on nails, waiting to hear the decision regarding whether my Baby B in the NICU could join us.

Finally, the nurse came in and looked at me with a huge smile on her face: "I have great news. You and both of your babies are free to go home." As I released the breath that I had been holding since she entered my room, tears of joy filled my eyes. I could hold my Baby B as much as I wanted and begin the bonding process with him.

Reality finally began to set in when we made it home. It helped that my mom, a sister, and the twins' father were there initially to help with the transition. Within the first four weeks we had a pretty good routine in place. The twins were on the same schedule when it came to food and sleep time. Every two hours Baby B would typically be the one to wake up ready to eat, and approximately two minutes later, Baby A would begin to squirm around indicating it was time for his feeding. In addition to getting these babies on a schedule, I had to figure out how I could balance my online school semester which was ending once Christmas break arrived. We had established a normal cadence so that I could do my schoolwork while also taking care of my newborns: feed babies every two hours, burp babies, change their diapers, rock them to sleep, lay babies down for a nap and repeat until I approached the end of my class day around 4:30pm.

After that, the babies had my complete attention until I bathed them and put them down for the night. Instead of waking up every two hours at this point, it expanded to every 4-5 hours. While the boys were sleeping, I would complete any open assignments from the day. My mom and sister had since returned home to Milwaukee to get back to their normal day to day lives.

Fast forward to November 19th - the day of devastation that almost caused me to lose my mind. It started like any other day. What made this day a little different was the fact that the twins had their first doctor's appointment, 6 weeks since leaving the hospital. I had already laid out their clothes out the night before and arranged for the taxi to pick us up. I did not have a vehicle of my own the entire time I attended Arizona State University, which made things quite challenging once I had to get around with infant twins. I had just finished a normal round of feed baby, burp baby, change diapers, rock baby to sleep and lay baby down for a nap. Given our appointment was in another four hours, I knew exactly how much time I had to spare to stick to the boys' schedule and make it to their doctor's appointment on time. I went to pick up Baby A and as I placed him in my hands, there was a gush of fear that ran from the top of my head to the soles of my feet. It felt as if his tiny little body had gone limp and appeared lifeless. I yelled at the top of my lungs "Call 911! Something is wrong with my baby!" into the silence.

I began to rub baby A's face and talk to him as we waited on the paramedics to arrive. What was only a 7-10-minute wait felt like an eternity. As I touched his face and spoke to him, he slowly opened his eyes. As I looked at him, his eyes were twitching side-to-side. I knew from the depths of my soul that something was drastically wrong. There was a loud heavy knock on the door and the paramedics rushed in. I handed my baby to them, and they began to do their normal protocol checks. Checking his heart rate, listening to his lungs, and checking his eyes to see if his pupils were dilatated. All those initial checks were normal, but I insisted that my baby be taken into the emergency room because I knew something was wrong. Since my baby was only six weeks old, they obliged and agreed to bring him in for observation.

I rode in the back of the ambulance with my baby. My heart was sitting in the pit of my stomach as I replay over and over in my head those moments before when my baby's body went limp in my hands. What could possibly be wrong? We were preparing to see his pediatrician today. Why would this happen now? If I have to stay in the hospital with baby 'A,' who was going to care for my other newborn? The whole incident felt like a nightmare that I desperately wanted to wake up from.

We arrived at the hospital, and I followed the stretcher as it exited the rear doors of the ambulance. I took a deep breath and prayed that everything would be okay. As I walked through these long white halls, it appeared as if I was entering a deeper, darker dimension of this horror that I had unwillingly entered 30 minutes prior as I saw my baby's life flash before my eyes. It felt like I was watching a movie of what was happening to me and my baby, unable to imagine being in this place.

They took us into one of the emergency rooms where we waited for about a half hour before the on-call doctor came in to check my baby's vitals and screen him. During the wait, I held my baby, willing his little eyes to open again, praying that everything was going to be okay.

The doctor entered the room with a look on his face as if he had already come up with a prognosis before even laying eyes on my baby. In a very nonchalant manner, he asked me to explain what had happened. I began to tear up as I explained to him my morning encounter that scared the life out of me. Still in shock, I laid my baby on the table for him to perform and examination. He checked my baby for what seemed like no longer than two minutes and left the room while saying something to the effect of "we'll run some tests." I yelled after him, "Something isn't right, why would my baby eyes be twitching like this." "We'll run a test for RSV," he responds. There I was, a young mother not knowing what RSV was but trusting that the doctor had my baby's best interest in mind.

About fifteen minutes after the doctor left the room, there was another episode that felt as if my baby's body went limp again. I frantically yelled for a nurse. "Help!! There is something wrong with my baby!!" The nurses came rushing in to check on him, and when they looked him over, they said they did not see anything wrong. They were waiting for the doctor to complete the testing orders. After about five minutes, they left the room. How could we be in the emergency room, and still not get the help that we needed?

Out of desperation, I grabbed my phone and called my children's pediatrician to see if he could provide some help. I let the receptionist know who answered the phone that this was an emergency and that I needed to talk to the pediatrician immediately. They quickly connected me with him and I began to relay my traumatic morning for the third time, now with the additional information that we were in the emergency room, and that I did not feel like we were getting the care that we deserved. After explaining the harrowing story to him he explained that they were checking for the wrong thing.

"This doesn't sound like RSV to me," he said. "They need to do a CAT scan because it sounds like some neurological is going on with the twitching of the eyes."

I thanked him for his help and rushed off to page the nurse to share what my baby's pediatrician had suggested. The response was not one of gratitude but of disbelief that I had even called my baby's pediatrician. She said she will check with the doctor on call since he is the person to make the call on what treatment and tests will be run." Five minutes later the nurse returned with a bottle in her left hand for my baby and stated the doctor would be returning to check on my baby once he finished his rounds.

At this point, I realized that they had not taken seriously the message that I relayed from my baby's pediatrician. She asked if it was okay for her to give him his feeding and I agreed, thinking to myself this would give me a moment to breathe and collect my thoughts. My baby appeared to be drinking the first two ounces just fine, she leant him forward to burb between every two ounces. Suddenly, he began to vomit as if he was a human water-foundation. This is when reality set in for the emergency staff and they finally began to handle us as if there was an emergency. We had been at the hospital for 2-3 hours and hadn't received proper care until then.

The nurse ran out of the room frantically with my baby in her hands saying, "code blue" and "this baby needs some help." This was the point where everything began to feel like a blur. I could not wrap my head around me holding my baby in my arms for one minute, the next me letting a nurse feed him, and the next him being rushed out of the room to receive emergency care. I stood in the dim-lit room all by myself, left to do the only thing in my power - to pray. Once I had the strength to move my legs and trace the steps that they had just taken since they rushed out of the room with my baby boy, I left the room looking frantically from left to right asking out loud about my baby. Where was he? A nurse that I had not yet interacted with told me she would go find the doctor and have him come right away.

The doctor returned to the room with a grim look on his face and said the dreadful words "please sit down." I slowly sat down on the edge of the emergency room bed, trying to keep my composure so that I could clearly hear what this doctor had to say. The first words out of his mouth were "things are not looking good." The more he talked, the deeper my heart fell in my stomach.

"Your baby has had a stroke and he has a lot of bleeding on his brain. We have him on a ventilator and are waiting on the neurosurgeon to arrive to let us know if brain surgery is needed."

The tears began to flow uncontrollably as my heart began to break one piece at a time. This was a moment of utter devastation. All I could get out of my mouth in response through the shakiness and crackling of my voice was "I want to see my baby."

"Once things are a little more stabilized, we will take you to his room in the ICU," said the doctor.

As soon as he left the emergency room that we were placed in per our arrival to the hospital, I fell to my knees and began to pray as I sobbed uncontrollably. I heard a small, still voice tell me, "Everything is going to be okay, do not be moved by what you see or hear." In that instant, an unusual peace came over me and although my baby's fate was unknown, there was a tiny part of me—about the size of a mustard seed—that believed what that still voice said. I slowly began to get up off the ground as I wiped the river of tears off my face. I sat back on the edge of the bed again in utter disbelief as a million thoughts began to cycle through my head. The doctor returned to my room 30 minutes later to tell me that they were going to take me to see my baby.

When I entered the ICU and saw tubes and wiring connected to my baby's little body, I was overwhelmed with tears again. It is one thing to hear a prognosis and an entirely different thing to see that prognosis up close and personal. As I looked at him through the glass incubator, I felt that I had to keep my composure the best I knew how because I knew he could sense that I was in the room. He needed to preserve all the strength he had to make it through his now two-week stay in the hospital that was ahead of him. I began to play back the words of that peaceful voice that spoke to me like a mantra. "Everything is going to be okay, do not be moved by what you see or hear."

After about an hour, I left the room to figure out what to do about my other newborn who was being watched by a friend temporally during this "quick" visit to the emergency room. I made some phone calls to my mother and aunt to coordinate the care that would be needed for baby 'B' while I stayed close to be 'A' as we navigated this time of uncertainty and called a cab to go grab clothes for the next couple days at the hospital. With one newborn in an emergency room incubator, and one needing to be cared for at home, how could I be at two places at once? I wondered how long I would be separated from both of my babies.

It could not have been more than fifteen minutes after making it back to my house that I received a knock on the door. This was really surprising because I definitely was not expecting anyone, not to mention I was nowhere near being mentally prepared to deal with anyone. I opened the door to find a man and a woman standing in front of me with CPS (Child Protective Services) badges asking if they could come in. Neither knowing my rights nor why they were even at my house, I invited them inside. As they stepped into the foyer and the door closed behind them, they explained that they know things are pretty serious with my baby. That the doctors have given him 24 hours to live. If he lived, he would be in persistent vegetative state, causes include head trauma or brain damage from an illness or stroke. They said they were at my home because someone from the hospital suspected foul play caused this to happen to my baby boy.

"We're going to need you to turn over temporary rights of both children until we can clear you."

Absolutely stunned, completely heartbroken, utterly distraught and devastated by this proclamation, the tears began to flow uncontrollably again. There were so many things wrong. Why was I hearing for the first time that my baby could have only 24 hours to live from a CPS worker and not the doctor? Who would even insinuate from the hospital that I would cause any harm to my baby, whom I absolutely adored? Throughout this traumatic ordeal, I had been the biggest advocate for my baby. If I had not called his pediatrician while in the emergency room, who knows what would have happened?

Why would I have to turn the rights of my babies - including the one who has nothing to do with this situation- over to CPS? No one had graced me with the smallest expression of empathy. I was facing two different, crushing losses at the same time: losing one baby's life, and custody of the other. This was the moment where utter and complete devastation washed over me. I was going to lose my mind.

My faith was truly the only thing that sustained me during this traumatic and unbelievably low time. I had to trust and rely on something bigger than myself to get through. In the end, my baby did not need brain surgery, we were released from the hospital after exactly two weeks, and the neurologist had to retract his diagnosis of my son ending up with severe brain damage.

I still was forced unjustly to deal with the CPS monitoring my daily life for six months with no just cause. The case was dropped because, of course, there was no evidence of foul play or of either one of my babies being in any danger.

Miraculously, and despite this traumatic experience, I never stopped going to engineering school and completed my degree. Today my twins are thriving, healthy 14-year-old teenagers. My son who at six weeks old had a stroke does require occupational, physical and speech therapy but it has not stopped him from being an active, sports-playing teenager.

That still, resounding voice that got me through an unfathomably trying moment was right: everything is okay. This experience taught me how to apply my faith in other areas of my life. not be moved by what I hear or see and trust myself and that gentle voice on the inside.

> **There were three key guiding principles that carried me through this soul shattering event: faith, perseverance, and positivity.**

My faith was the anchor that kept me on solid ground when I felt myself sinking into the depths of the sea. At that darkest moment in my experience, I felt there were only two options for me: I could crumble and be swallowed up in sorrow or I could cling to something bigger than myself. The someone who created the universe who I call Yahweh and has many names, who tells the sun to rise and set every day, and who knew me before I was even in my mother's womb. Not only do it was faith that sustained me, but it was the very thing that saved my baby as well.

Perseverance, to keep pushing and moving forward despite the moments of uncertainty and the challenges I faced. I continued my college work without missing one beat during that entire traumatic time. When I think about how I made it through, I am still in awe that experience did not send me on a different life trajectory, giving up on my dreams of obtaining my Engineering' degree.

How does one persevere? By facing every moment and reminding oneself that getting to the other side of a challenge is worth the reward. Casting down your fears and ruminating on the negative thoughts of what could potentially go wrong in your pursuit of obtaining your goals. Eventually, when you say that to yourself enough, you'll begin to believe it from the depths of your being. Once you believe it, the next step is actualization – making it happen.

This last guiding principle is the consistent thread through each story that I share in this book. Our brains are wired to put more weight on negative experiences, referred to as negativity bias. This is a great trait when it comes to addressing potential threats or danger, but it can be catastrophic if it is misplaced and directed to an encounter that is an opportunity to grow.

Since we naturally focus on negative things and experiences, we must re-program our brains to change the way we approach things.

The things we dwell on are the things that we end up manifesting. If my life isn't in immediate danger, what value does it add to continuously focus on the negative things around me? No value at all. It just sends you down a sink hole that keeps you from personal growth and enjoying the moment. I know that you have probably heard of the phrase "Debbie Downer." For those who have not, this phrase is used colloquially to refer to a person who always sees the negative side of every situation. There is nothing positive that they have to say. They have something negative to say about everyone and everything. This person's energy is negative, and it brings you down just by being around them. If we are not intentional about fighting this negativity bias, we can become our own "Debbie Downer" causing us to manifest the very things that we do not desire to obtain.

Despite how negative a situation is that I encounter, I try to find a positive perspective. Here are a couple of real-life examples:

- My six-week-old baby had a major stroke that affected the right side of his body, his prognosis was that he would live 24 hours or become severely brain damaged, and I was distraught. This was truly a traumatic experience, but instead of me continuing to relive the negative experience, I have chosen to focus on my victories from this situation.

- My baby survived a traumatic experience, which truly shows how strong he is. This experience showed me how fragile life is and how important it is to treasure every moment. I thank God that at the point when I thought I would lose my mind, Yahweh saved me.

No matter what type of experience we have or what challenges we go through, we can choose to find a positive perspective. Homing in on the silver-lining ("something good that can be found in a bad situation") and only speaking words of positivity over your situation. Sometimes we underestimate the power associated with the words that we speak.

Choosing to focus on the positive perspective sets you free

from the agony of the experience. It does not change the experience itself, and it is okay to feel sad, angry, or scared. But it provides a way to get you through it, and I would even attest that it aids you in your healing process. We have so many things to be grateful for—I challenge you to find moments in every experience to celebrate.

What I have realized is that there comes a point in our lives that we have to believe in something greater than ourselves. There are situations that come our way that we absolutely have no control over. At that moment we're left with a few options: throw in the towel and just say forget everything or put your trust in something bigger than yourself and believe that despite how things turn out in that moment everything will work together for your good. For me, it's been my faith in God that has carried me in those really dark moments.

Chapter One: Reflection Exercise

Guiding principles: Faith, Perseverance, Positivity.

Think of a time when you felt defeated, devastated or it seemed that you had no control over a difficult situation. Why were those moments defeating/devastating? How did you process the defeat/devastation? What did you learn about yourself during that trying time? How have those moments of defeat/devastation shaped the person that you are today? How could you have used any or all of the above principles to get through it?

CHAPTER TWO
IMPOSTER SYNDROME:
YOU HAVE NO ROOM IN MY LIFE

As I look back over my life, there were many points where I did not feel worthy and quite frankly did not know who I truly was. I let the people around me control the narrative of who I was and who I would grow up to be, that included family, friends, classmates and members within the community.

Sometimes I don't feel like there is enough emphasis put on the impact that your environment has on shaping the person that you become. At the age of seven, I made the decision that my life would be different than the everyday experience of poverty, where the norm in the community was families on welfare, section-8, energy-assistance, free school meals and community-sponsored summer programs. As I fought to break the barriers that I was born into, I was faced with opposition that made me question whether I deserved to dream bigger and whether it was obtainable.

Until my late twenties, I felt like an outsider in most situations in which I found myself because of my will to push beyond my roots in poverty, the biases and the stereotypes inherited simply because of my background. Imposter syndrome became this pervasive feeling that I was a fraud, that I did not belong where I was or strove to be, or that I did not deserve to sit in rooms in which I had rightly earned a seat at the table. Especially coming from a marginalized group, the weight of imposter syndrome seems heavier as there are multiple layers of breakthrough needed. In my case: first-generation college graduate, African American woman, single parent household, single parent, first and only engineer in my family and first one to navigate my career in corporate America.

Once I learned of imposter syndrome, I could finally put a name to what I had been experiencing at various points throughout my life.

Let me start with my first real experience with Imposter Syndrome, engineering school at a predominately white university. This is after already having to combat my doubts and fears around whether I had what it took to make it in college, let alone succeed in engineering school. I am the first and only engineer in my entire family on both my maternal and paternal side. I remember the first class, "Intro to Engineering." The lecture hall held three hundred other students. As I glanced across the room, from left to right, then all around, there was no other person there who looked like me. I leaned back in my chair and an overwhelming sense of fear came over me. Thinking to myself...

"Do I deserve to be in this room?"

"Will I measure up to the standard that was expected of me to be successful in engineering school?"

"Since there is absolutely no one that looks like me in the room, do I belong here?"

This experience was the beginning of many experiences of becoming entangled in the web of imposter syndrome.

My journey through engineering school was far from the "typical experience" of having a clear plan of what school would entail and finishing my degree in 4-5 years. Instead, I met with my academic advisor at the beginning and end of each semester, reassessing what classes I needed to pursue next as I took baby steps towards the finish line. I was committed obtaining to my goal of completing this degree at all costs, if that meant it would take a lifetime for me to finish. After having my twins, I doubled down on my pursuit because they deserve nothing but the best.

There were layers of depth to my imposter syndrome, each layer rooted in my experiences and the low regard that I had of my worth. A lack of self-worth is at the root of feeling like an imposter, thinking that you do not belong in spaces where you have demonstrated competencies and actually deserve to be in the 'room' because of your education and/or experiences. Now I understand that there are instances where those who have earned a seat at the table do not actually get the opportunity to sit there due to racism, sexism or systematic bias. This topic would warrant its own book. I will focus on sharing some of the challenges I faced when making the transition from engineering school to "Corporate America."

Corporate America is where I realized the severity of imposter syndrome and how it kept me for a long time from bringing my whole self to work and being true to the real me—the me that shows up with my close family and friends. The me that does not second guess what comes out of my mouth when I know that I am speaking truly. The me who does not feel judged simply because my thoughts and viewpoints are different. The me who does not have to change the inflections in my voice so that I sound like those who make up the majority in the room. The me who accepts all of me; the inner fashionista, the mood-inspired hair changer, the nerd who happens to have swagger and the influential, creative thinker.

Back to my engineering school experience for a moment. There were various points in that 8-year journey when I was unsure if I would make it through or not. It was taxing at times to enter a room where there was literally no one that looked like me or shared my life experiences. Walking into my 1st day of Physics I, looking around the room where no one resembled me not even the professor was daunting. Fear attempting to engulf me as I percolate on what it would take to be successful in this class. Would my classmates want to partner with me and form study groups? Would I even have time to meet with my peers given the responsibility that I have at home taking care of two small children? I felt as if I was behind the curve, as if my peers' upbringing had prepared them to sit in the classroom and succeed. I did not attend private schools throughout my childhood nor come from a family were college preparation started even before I was born. Coming from an under-served community where the term engineer was not even used, in addition to no one in my circle of friends or family who could help show me the ropes, I had to work extremely hard for every grade that I received. In addition to feeling like I had to work twice as hard as those unlike me, there were even some professors who made me feel as if I didn't belong. They minimized my efforts and responded to my questions implying that I did not have what it took to complete the program.

What they didn't realize is that I have always used other peoples' doubt about me as fuel in the fire to go after my dreams and aspirations even harder.

When I feel or hear doubt projected on me, my immediate response internally is "I can show you better than I can tell you. Just watch me.

I cannot deny that there were times when I questioned myself, thinking, "Were they right about me not having what it takes to succeed?" Especially those moments in my journey where I failed a couple of classes multiple times. I had to take Calculus II and Physics II several times. This took perseverance. At the same time, failing these classes validated my feelings of being a fraud and left me feeling bound by imposter syndrome.

Even after completing my engineering program despite how challenging, it, was, the impact of imposter syndrome carried over to the next phase of my life, entering Corporate America. My first job post-graduation was at a manufacturing company where I was the first female engineer that the company had ever hired. Talk about questioning whether I belonged or not! Much like engineering school, this was a male-dominated environment. I believe that my saving grace in being successful in that environment had everything to do with me saying 'yes' to a pilot project that eventually turned into a new line of business for the organization.

This was my chance to show that I had the ability to thrive in this environment and validate that I deserved to be in my role. Feeling again the need to be validated by those around me was something that also kept me bound by imposter syndrome. Giving up the need to seek validation from others was a critical piece of breaking free from imposter syndrome. Reality set in when I realized the validation that I was getting from the men about how well I was doing on the pilot project had little meaning in the grand scheme of things. After completing the multi-dimensional, complex, and high liability pilot project that was so successful that the customer decided to utilize the company to build more products, my leadership brought in a white man, had me train him, and then appointed him my supervisor.

This experience did have two equal and opposite effects: it added another badge to my imposter syndrome vest while at the same time sparking a fire inside of me to never accept the status quo. It was vexing because on one hand I was questioning whether I belonged and grilling myself on what things I could have done differently to prove I was worthy of that supervisor role; on the other hand, the innermost part of me knew that not only was I worthy of the role but that I deserved it. I was the one who put the blood, sweat and tears - pulling all-nighters to read blueprints and spec documents to ensure that the product complied with regulatory requirements. My core inner self won, and instead of staying in a toxic environment that fed on self-doubt and imposter syndrome, I decided to leave the organization. My attempts to blend in with "the engineering boys club" tarnished the self-confidence that I had found through my accomplishments as an engineer.

The second industry that I transitioned to came with its own set of challenges. Being in a new company where I technically did not have much experience in the industry had imposter syndrome rearing its ugly head yet again. Although I was hired to fulfill a role that I was capable of, there was an internal battle going on inside me about whether I truly deserved to be there. As I continued to navigate the space, I earned recognition and awards for operational excellence, which gave me more confidence that I deserved to be there. However, despite how well I was doing my job, I did not feel like I was truly bringing my authentic self to work. I brought a piece of me that I thought would be accepted in Corporate America.

Yet again, I found myself in a situation where I was one of the few people that looked like me, and I felt like I had to downplay who I was to be accepted. Knowing that, ultimately, the majority of the people in the room were those who would be making decisions about my performance and compensation, I felt pressure to engage with them in a manner to which they were accustomed. This required me to observe their norms and make sure that I incorporated them in my day-to-day interactions. Wear your hair this way, these clothes are perceived that way. Make sure that you do not show emotions while speaking, you don't want to come across as overbearing or validating the stereotypes that they already have about Black women. Don't buck against the norm too much or else you will be seen as someone who is not a team player or "argumentative." The list goes on.

Just Imagine having to perform your job to the highest standard of excellence while also dealing with the emotional baggage of sorting through and performing the "norms." It is exhausting. How can you bring the best version of yourself to your work in this manner? What kept me going through this time were those few leaders who saw the things that were different about me were part of my true value and afforded me opportunities to leverage my talents. Unfortunately, those same leaders were not in my direct leadership chain. Another layer of mental exhaustion was fighting against egos of leaders who did not recognize that I had more to offer than simply the job that I was hired to perform. I have always been a "Big-Picture" thinker, once I master one area, I intentionally go on a problem-solving quest to see where there are connection points in other parts of the business. In addition, finding opportunities to positively impact the broader 'Employee Experience' whether it pertained to philanthropy or Diversity Equity and Inclusion (DEI) initiatives.

There were several more encounters that caused me to unnecessarily question things about myself, emboldening my imposter syndrome and increasing my self-doubt. My industry switch was another moment that emboldened my imposter syndrome and increased my self-doubt. I was pursuing a role in a new region that the company had recently opened. This role was technically the exact same role that I was already doing but in a different location and reporting to a different manager. After applying for the role, I was shocked to find out that my current manager was on the interviewing team for this new role. This sent me into a tailspin! A real breach of trust – not to mention a clear conflict of interest and misuse of power as I know my current manager did not want me to leave the team. Unsurprisingly, I was not selected for the new role without explanation besides what I knew in my heart as I was excelling in my current role. The only explanation I could produce was my manager's lack of maturity, and a desire to preserve her team's success at any cost. She used her power over me to protect herself at all costs with complete disregard for my career development. After receiving that 'no,' I was disappointed, disillusioned, and angry thinking that I didn't get the role because I wasn't good enough then later knowing the true story. Even after knowing the truth about the entire situation, that 'rejection' played into my natural imposter syndrome tendency and my response was to question everything about myself, again.

"Maybe I wasn't ready?"

"Maybe I didn't meet the requirements?"

"Maybe I'm just not enough."

These are examples of the lies that imposter syndrome will encourage you to tell yourself: you're not enough, you need more of this or that, you still have more to prove, everything you've done up to this point means nothing. This was a watershed moment for me. Instead of becoming consumed in this quicksand of "not enough," I decided to use this opportunity as fuel to position myself in a way where people would not be able to say that I did not meet the criteria. Shortly after this experience I decided to go back to school to get my MBA with a focus on leadership. Obtaining the skillset and tools to be a better leader than those I had personally experienced and that I felt had failed miserably. I had learned that there was a difference between managers and leaders.

I came to peace with the situation when the hiring manager for the new role I had interviewed apologized to me. She felt ashamed because she knew that the only reason, I was rejected for that position was because my then manager did not want to lose me from her team. I was angry, but at peace knowing that not getting the role had nothing to do with whether I was "enough" and everything to do with a manager who chose to abuse her power. I did not stay in that role too much longer before finding my way back to school. One of the positive outcomes from this unfair situation was that it prompted me to go back to school and obtain my MBA, which helped me become better positioned for my future, holding both an Engineering degree and an MBA.

It was as if I had entered a whole new world after making my third career pivot into the technology sector. As I walked around my new 502-acre work campus, everywhere that I turned there were people confident and comfortable with being themselves. There was a woman with green and pink hair wearing the most casual clothing that I've ever seen in the workplace. There were men with blue hair, both arm sleeves covered in tattoos, long hair and bulky jewelry adorning on their wrists. I could not believe my eyes, especially after starting out in an industry that was very conservative. Business casual was the normal attire. Someone coming in with any other hair outside of the acceptable norm would probably have been escorted out of the building. Exposure to this environment removed a layer of my imposter syndrome almost immediately. This environment was conducive to me showing up physically the way that I wanted to, no longer feeling the pressure to adhere to homogeneity.

For the first month, every day was a new adventure, picking attire that was bright in color and accessorized in a way that only I could assess whether the environment was really amenable to me showing up as "myself." The multifaceted version of myself showing up as sophisticated with a hint of spice or sporty with a hint of sass. Anyone who really knows me will acknowledge that I have a love for fashion and all things clothes, shoes, and accessories. After the first 30 days of me testing the environment, it turned out to be true. I could show up in a way that was authentic to who I truly am. How many of you have minimized who you are in hopes of not being rejected in environments where you desired to be accepted? Afraid that if you are not accepted it could jeopardize your livelihood or your next promotion? When we don't show up in a way that is true and authentic to ourselves, we tell imposter syndrome 'you have room in our lives.'

Let's declare that imposter syndrome has no room in our lives. Say it with me: "Imposter syndrome, I break your chains that have kept me from showing up as my authentic self in every environment —you have no room in my life!!"

This first layer of imposter syndrome that I shed set the stage for my two and a half-year journey to being set completely free. I realized that the roots of imposter syndrome run deep and were intertwined with almost every area of my life: my job, relationships, social environments, and how I showed up at public gatherings. The journey was like peeling layers of an onion to get to the core, and once I got to the core, I was able to be free from these false perceptions of myself. There were multiple moments of breakthrough that I encountered and conquered that brought me to where I am now. Some moments were harder than others, and I would like to share one more experience that I consider my "pivotal peak" with the encounter that brought me to the core of this onion. This encounter was directly tied to my self-worth, which is the very thing that imposter syndrome aims to assault.

After about four months into the tech industry while doing one of the things I absolutely love to do, pouring into others through mentorship, I discovered that I was under-leveled when I was hired into the organization. In other words, I was hired at a lower level and lower pay than is commensurate with my education and experience, with no opportunity to negotiate. At this point I reflected on my career and realized that this was a common theme that showed up in my experience with previous industries as well. Often, I was the most "qualified" when considering my education and experience, but my pay and titles never reflected this.

Systemic bias, unconscious bias, and racism are contributors to imposter syndrome, these contributors are often felt first and sometimes not seen by those who are not directly impacted by its sting. If a person is already battling with themselves on whether they are "worthy" to be in a 'room' and then you couple that with being placed in environments where the soundwaves in the room are sending the same message "You are not enough and you don't belong here," the impact of imposter syndrome is compounded. Corporate America was not designed to allow someone who fits my persona to have a seat at the "big" table where decisions are being made. The "big" table is the space where the "true leaders" gather and make important strategic decisions about the business. These people have titles like manager, director, general manager, vice president, C-suite officer, and board member. These people are those who have the power to hire, fire, establish culture and values, and to make the institutional change needed to break the cycle of systemic bias that has kept certain people —especially African American/Black women—from having access to the "big table."

I'm an African American/Black woman who grew up in poverty, a first-generation college graduate, and a Corporate America qualified professional. A never-married single mother to teenage twin boys, who has obtained both a degree in Engineering with a minor in African American Studies and a Master of Business Administration. I have experience in four major industries, working across over seven different disciplines. If I add my educational experience, it is five different industries. Recently in a conversation with a recruiter after going over my experience she said, "I consider you to be multi-lingual with your ability to pivot into multiple disciplines." As I pondered this, I decided to coin the word," multi-biz-lingual," the ability to shift between multiple business areas and make strategic impact.

I share all of that to say that there is no logical reason that would justify why I and others like me would not have a seat at the "big" tables by now. I have been in countless situations where the people at the "big" table were there because of their connections and/or sponsored by other people of power that look like them, unilaterally making space at the table for them.

Is it fair that I should be excluded because I lack the "right" connections that were established through generational relationships of being in Corporate America? I am the first in my family to enter that realm. Or is it because if someone who looks like me obtains access to the "big" table they are often afraid to make space there for others that look like them lest be perceived as showing favoritism to those from their background? No. The irony is that the others who are from the majority and occupy most of the power and the seats at the "big" table are not subjected to that level or fear, or that type of scrutiny because it is assumed that they belong there. Things have to change!

I am thankful for the allies outside of the African American/Black Community who have decided to stand up and say this systemic racism is not acceptable, and mandate that these systems change. This lifts some of the weight off the shoulders of a community that is already burdened by so many other things, which makes me sometimes feel like I am skating uphill on a sheet of ice. A nearly impossible challenge to conquer without the proper equipment of which I will elaborate more in Chapter Four, "The shackles of poverty still remain...."

The events of 2020 exposed how African American/Black communities have been systemically oppressed and marginalized across the education system, prison system, justice system, health-care system—and Corporate America.

I realized that if I did not recognize my worth and if I did not advocate for myself, then who would? I cannot expect something from others that I was unable to give to myself first. Embarking on this journey of discovering my own self-worth and standing up unapologetically to be an advocate for myself came with a lot of tears. It was grueling. As I discovered where my self-worth had been damaged, the tears and knowing that Yahweh was with me in those moments were the only things that consoled me. It was hard to face the fact that I would let others walk up-and-down the front and back of me, leaving me bruised and wounded, setting a standard to just accept anyway somebody wanted to treat me. Somewhere along the journey, accepting the crumbs that someone left with a smile became my normal. During my journey of healing and restoring my self-worth, I fought to keep a positive perspective and forgive myself for not advocating for my worth sooner.

I emerged with a newfound confidence, and I gained the strength to go up the leadership chain seeking answers on why and how I was able to come into the organization under-leveled. My boldness came as a surprise to some and for others the level of respect they had for me increased. Several people acknowledged that how I was brought into the company did not match my level of skill and experience; however, they were not willing to rectify the wrong at that moment. I did what I felt like was my only option—I left the organization.

With this decision, came three major accomplishments:

1. My self-worth was restored—and I vowed to keep it intact.
2. For the first time, I was a real advocate for myself
3. I broke free from imposter syndrome and could say with great conviction, "Imposter syndrome! You have no room in my life!"

There were four guiding principles that carried me through this journey: remaining determined, staying agile, discovering identity, and maintaining a positive perspective.

Keeping my eye on the promise that I made to my 7-year-old-self that my life would be different than what I saw around me growing up required me to remain focused and determined to obtain those dreams. We must be laser-focused when striving for those larger-than-life milestones.

Agility has been essential in making major pivots in my life, when necessary, from switching roles to switching industries. Being agile sometimes requires you to be comfortable with being uncomfortable. I have found that on the other side of my most uncomfortable moments came my greatest rewards.

Identity. This is the big rock that we have to turn over. Discovering your identity is directly connected to uncovering your purpose. When we do not know who we truly are, we are aimlessly roaming this earth, vainly seeking a purpose which we cannot understand. I found my true identity through anchoring to something bigger than myself, for me that was allowing Yahweh to have complete access to my life and showing me through words or visions who I truly am. Not coming into agreement with the words from critics and not letting my environments dictate who I am or who I'm supposed to become.

Maintaining a positive perspective through these experiences was especially important. Had I not had the ability to shift the way that I perceived situations in the moment, I could very well be a rightfully angry person with a chip on my shoulder. Instead, I have used those not-so-great moments as fuel to be an even stronger advocate for myself and others.

That strategy has served me well. Some of the wrongs

along my career journey have been made right. I now have a "seat at the table." After obtaining this "seat," I make the commitment to continue to show up as my authentic self and immediately refute imposter syndrome when it rears its head.

Chapter Two: Reflection Exercise

Guiding principles: Determination, Agility, Identity, Positivity.

Initiate a conversation with oneself. This exercise will require you to take a hard look at yourself and determine whether you have showed up as your true authentic self. Do you hold back who you are based on the rooms you enter because you are more concerned about being accepted than showing the world who you really are? I mean the "you" who don't have a care in the world, who chooses to love self unconditionally despite those who may fall by the wayside. The "you" who accepts the scars, marks, blemished skin, wrinkles, stretch marks and can still look at yourself in the mirror and say, "I'm beautiful and I love everything about me". I commit to accept the things that I can't change and make a conscious effort to rectify the things that I can control.

Create a list of 10-12 affirmations that you will speak over yourself every day for the next 3 months. At the end of the 3 months assess whether you are living out the affirmations that you've spoken about yourself. If you have, come up with a new list as we all should be our own greatest cheerleader.

CHAPTER THREE
THE HEARTBREAK(S) SHOWED ME MY WORTH

Like many of you, I have experienced my share of heartbreak, ranging across the spectrum of relationships. As I reflect over these encounters, a common thread rings true: every heartbreak was connected to an unfulfilled expectation. Let me start with the most prominent relationship, the one with my father, or, rather, my absent father. This relationship set the stage for how I interacted with men, desiring from them more than they were willing to give, either because they did not know how to love someone outside of themselves or simply because they didn't want to.

As I mentioned earlier in this book, I grew up in a single parent household where I was one of four children. I am the only child that my parents had together, though I have siblings from both sides. The irony is that my absentee father was present for seven years prior to me being conceived but decided not to be present shortly after finding out that my mother was pregnant. He stayed around long enough to plant the seed that helped create me and disappeared like the sun does at dawn.

As a young girl, I would often daydream about what it would be like having my father around. It would break my heart to watch other children interact with their fathers, because on the inside I thought that I was really a "daddy's girl." These thoughts were often shattered the moment I drifted out of my daydreams and came back to reality. I always wondered what would make a man leave his child who he helped bring into the world and then never look back. To miss the special milestones, like experiencing my first words or watching me transition from baby to toddler to adolescent to adult. What about the responsibility of a father to protect, love and be the first man to tell his daughter that she is beautiful? His absence left a gaping hole in my heart that was later filled by all the wrong kind of men. The hole contained my uncertainty around my self-worth, confidence in myself, and how I perceived love.

I lost my uncle unexpectedly. He was like a father to me, and he showed me the love that his brother (my father) was not capable of giving. It left a huge hole in my heart and still brings me to tears when I think about the fact that he is no longer here physically. I chose to celebrate that he was an amazing man who spoke words of affirmation over me every chance that he could. The words that he spoke to me still live on and have carried me through some dark days. Even in his absence, I feel that I have an angel that is always watching over me. I am grateful for the moments that we shared and appreciate the time that we had together.

I did not meet my absentee father in person until I was 34 years old, by this time having experienced three major heartbreaks outside of the original one that he had caused. And to make matters worse, I experienced another major heartbreak with him only four months after our first meeting. As I sat across a table from him, he held a baby boy in his hand, the son of his wife that he helped raised while abandoning his own. Filled with anticipation and anxiety, I asked him a question that I wanted to my whole life: "Why did you walk away from me and never think about being a part of my life?"

Well, he was not ready to answer that question and as anger covered his countenance, he responded, "The only child that I ever gave my love to is in the ground right now, and this child that I am holding will never have to worry about anything." In a state of utter disbelief, I had a feeling of rage and peace overtake me simultaneously. These words felt like someone had taken a machete and cut my heart into a million pieces. By the grace of God, I was able to calmly gather myself and make it to my car in the parking lot before the tears began to flow like Niagara Falls. I cried my entire drive home, to a point where the tears stung like fire as they left my eyes.

Through that pain, I made a promise to myself that I would never let him or anyone else hurt me in that manner again. Setting a boundary with anyone who does not recognize my worth, not placing people in positions in my life that they have not earned and removing misplaced expectations to those who don't understand the role they are meant to play in my life.

After the reunion with my father who I had always desired to have around, I thought he would come in and be the man that I daydreamed about as a little girl. He would be kind, considerate, loving and protective because that's what fathers "do" when it comes to their daughters. That expectation was shattered. I made the decision then that I was worth more than how I was treated on that day. It was almost a year and half after that experience before he reached out to me again, this time with an apology. I forgave him, but he would never have access to my heart in the way that he had in the past, and I found my peace that he could never be the father that I desired him to be. There was liberty and power that came with removing the expectations of him being a father to me, and just accepting him as a flawed human being as we all are.

May his soul rest in peace, a few months after the apology he transitioned to the afterlife. I can still remember the last conversation that we had four days prior to his transition so vividly, as it brought healing to the innermost part of me. It was almost like he knew that would be the last conversation that he would ever have, and he poured his heart out to me. "Baby girl, you are everything that I dreamed of and even more. Cannot believe it was possible to have someone so beautiful, kind, and intelligent come from me, especially with all the decisions that I made in life. I love you more than you'll ever know my love and I'm so proud of the woman that you've become! You will obtain everything that you set out to do, never stop believing. Forgive me for anything that I have done to hurt you and me not being there to watch every moment of your life."

At the end of the call, we told each other 'I love you' and when I hung up the phone I was overtaken with emotions. With every word that he spoke it was as if the small gaps that connected the puzzle pieces of my heart were being filled with superglue. Removing all of the residue that had taken residence in an attempt from keeping my heart from ever being completely healed from the first relationship that I desired from a man. In that moment, my desire to know what it felt like to be a "daddy's girl" was fulfilled. Even though it was just a moment that I truly experienced what it felt to feel the unconditional love of my father: about 345,600 seconds. The four days between this conversation with my father and his transition into eternal life was worth it. *As I write this, my tears begin to flow uncontrollably, writing one of the hardest parts of this book. I am grateful for my father's love that has set me free from the woes of not being properly loved by a man.*

Let's rewind the hand of time a bit as I walk through the heartbreaks that happened prior to the reunion with my father, where that gaping hole in my heart was an incubator for all things unwell and unsettled. The first man I will reference as my "Questionable First Love." I met him in the summer of my junior year in high school through a mutual friend. We were on a girls' trip to Memphis celebrating with my friend's childhood friends. This man was everything that I thought I wanted and needed, though little did I know that he would break my heart into a million pieces. But do we ever really know? Most times we go into relationships with our heart and minds wide open, ignoring all the red flags.

Young and naïve, I fell for this older man who presented himself as a man of God, and everything about our first encounter appeared to be magical. I left that trip from Memphis thinking that I met the man I would one day call my husband and have children with. He seemed to speak with so much clarity and there was conviction when he professed that I would be his wife. The next two years were bliss as we began to build on this long-distance relationship. This all shattered in a blink of an eye when I got the call from my best friend at that time telling me that my "Questionable First-love" was planning a wedding with someone else. I was distraught and devastated! I was also in sheer disbelief that the man who spoke sweet nothings in my ear for two years would betray me in this way with no remorse. After gaining control of the tears running uncontrollably down my face, my heart was torn into a million pieces, as if I could feel each piece rip, one piece at a time. I immediately began to question myself.

"Maybe you weren't woman enough for him given the age difference?"

"Your desire to save your body for your husband - maybe that was silly?"

"Is she prettier than me?"

"Is she smarter than me?"

"Maybe it's my fault since I made the decision to go to Arizona instead of Memphis?"

Each question running was another chisel at my confidence and trust in my heart. After a few weeks of marinating in this agony, my self-worth was as thin as a sheet of paper. I was left with emptiness. Uncertain if I would ever bounce back from this type of pain that I would not wish on anyone. At this point I just wanted the pain to go away, as I pushed my faith to the backburner. I was disappointed and could not understand why God would allow me to experience this terrible pain. Instead of taking time to heal and mend the million pieces of my heart that had fallen everywhere, I ran to the first person who gave me attention. Later, I realized that no one is exempt from experiencing negative things, but Yahweh does promise to work all things together for our good and that is truly my testimony. I also realized that most of the challenges that we experience in life are not only about us, but also for making a positive impact in other peoples' lives. For instance, had I not gone through all the challenges that I've been through up until this point, I would not have the words to write this book that I hope inspires you and gives you hope in your darkest moments.

The second man that I met after the heartbreak I refer to as "Mr. Rebound." I did not take the time to heal from my first relationship and ran to the first person who showed me attention. Everything about how I responded to this season of my life was out of character. I lost a part of myself in that previous relationship, and it reflected in my actions. Things happened extremely fast with "Mr. Rebound."

He was the rebound, but I ended up carrying the ball and the burden that came along with that. I met him at a friend's family reunion one weekend in Milwaukee, and about 8 weeks later he made a move to Arizona. He was there for about 6 months before I got pregnant with my twins. It felt like I was swept up in the middle of a tornado. I could see everything flying around me but did not know how to replant my feet on solid ground. At this point, I was still not addressing the hurt and brokenness from my previous relationship.

As the days went by, I separated from the real me, eventually arriving at a place where I no longer recognized myself. My mannerisms, language, desires and even my physical appearance changed for a few years. I was just existing and going through the motions. When I looked in the mirror, I couldn't recognize myself, even when I look at pictures from that chapter in my life my eyes begin to swell with tears. . Knowing that I lost the value and respect that I had for myself for a period of time is embarrassing and heart-wrenching. In those moments, I extend grace to myself and pivot my thoughts to focus on how I've grown since. We have to be intentional about not letting the decisions from our past begin a cycle of bondage that keeps us from becoming the best version of ourselves. I am so grateful that, in the midst of my season of emptiness, I did not forfeit my dream of obtaining my college degree. I've learned to extend grace to myself over –and over again and try to do the same when people are going through challenging times.

Shortly after the twins turned two years old, there was a fire that sparked inside of me, igniting a light in my heart that was once filled with darkness and emptiness. It was a combination of things: more time spent filling my spirit with the Bible, the realization that my children and I deserved nothing but the best and accepting the responsibility that my children needed a mother who was *whole*. Whole in mind, body, and soul, not damaging them unintentionally with the broken version of myself. I finally gained enough courage to tell their father that if he could not commit to being the man that I desire for the twins to grow up and be, then I preferred for us to go our separate ways.

The decision was hard because I never imagined that my children would grow up without their father living in the house with us. This was not how I envisioned my life playing out; however, it was necessary for my journey to create a whole and fulfilling life for my family. In order for us to show up and be the best for others, we must first be the best for ourselves. This is the reason that prioritizing self-care is a non-negotiable when you've been through a season of life where you feel you have lost yourself.

Self-care is taking care of your spiritual, physical, mental, and emotional well-being.

Although we were never married, the separation from the boys' father brought on a slew of opinions and comments from people looking in from the outside. None of that mattered because my peace, wholeness, and happiness were more important than others' views and opinions. It took about seven years after walking away from the situation for me to fully heal. During that 7-year period, there were high highs and low lows as I embarked on the journey of rediscovering myself.

Rediscovering myself as a single parent was not an easy task, requiring me to balance being a mother, a student, and a woman determined to achieve her dreams. I took it one day at a time and was intentional about uncovering the scabs that had infections festering under them. Those infections included insecurities, lack of confidence, little to no self-worth, and a permeating guilt for the decisions that I had made along the way because I never took the time to forgive myself. Eventually, I began to rise like a phoenix from the ashes. Not only was I restored, but I was an even better version of myself. My children were able to experience the fullness of their mother, a love that was not overshadowed by brokenness and guilt. I smiled more and my laughs were real, born from a place of wholeness. I deserved to become this version of myself, and my children deserved to experience it.

I began to pray regularly during this time of rediscovery about what was in store for myself and my children's futures. This included a petition for my future husband to find me and be my knight in shining armor, being everything that my children and I needed him to be. A man of valor, respect, integrity, family oriented, committed to building his family and loving us unconditionally. During this year period I had reoccurring dreams of a man that I will call "Mr. Dream Never Obtained." It was pretty surreal to see the same man in my dreams for several years and then to meet him in person. During our first interaction, it was as if we had known each other for a lifetime. Joy permeated my heart. This was the moment I had been waiting for after years of taking time to get the heart healing I needed before entering another relationship.

Again, things moved quickly, and we became a unit as he seemed to believe that I was the woman he had desired and was going to marry. We dated long distance for about two years before the dream that I once had turned into a nightmare. We made the agreement that there were things that we wanted to achieve before taking the relationship to the next level- falling in love, getting married, building together and growing my family with additional children. I would focus on finishing my MBA and he would work on building his own business. I kept my end of the bargain; however, he threw his end into the deep blue sea where it could no longer be found.

Instead of building his business, he was building a family with someone else and lying to me every step of the way. I was heartbroken when I found out that he had fathered a baby with another woman while we were dating. This experience took me back to my "Questionable First Love." There was absolutely nothing about the situation with "Mr. Dream Never Obtained" that I could understand.

That setback knocked the wind out of me, I could not believe that I had to experience deceit on this level again. The first with "Questionable First Love" marrying someone else while we were dating and "Mr. Dream Never Obtained" having a child while we were dating. I would be lying if I said that I did not question or blame myself for what happened in those relationships.

"Maybe you should have moved to the state that he was living in, and this wouldn't have happened."

"Maybe it's something about you that isn't desirable."

"Maybe you're not worthy enough to meet a man who

truly loves you unconditionally and is loyal."

Key lesson from this experience: success and healing are not linear. There will be setbacks, even when you think you have gotten to the next level of self-actualization. There will be ups and downs, and that is all part of the process.

I had to continue to cast down those lies in my mind. until I could believe I am worthy of love, respect, and loyalty. That I will be desirable to my future husband. That I will be an amazing wife who will help that man become the best version of himself.

Until then, I'm committed to loving myself unconditionally, extending grace to myself, not losing faith and knowing without a shadow of doubt my future husband will be certain about who I am and not take me for granted.

Whew, I know this chapter is loaded with some heavy stuff, sharing intimate details about the heartbreaks that eventually showed me my worth. Through these broken relationships I have been able to become clear about what I desire from myself and my future husband. I have also learned to not ignore the red flags—there were plenty in all three of these relationships that I ignored. I ignored them because I wanted the fairy tale story that so many girls and women desire: to be someone's wife – someone's life-partner, to love unconditionally, weather the ebbs-and-flows of the journey of growing together, fulfilling purpose and being my partner's greatest supporter.

I now refuse to accept anything that is less than what I deserve. Realizing that in each one of these relationships, the men were broken and incapable of giving me what they could not even give themselves: real love, respect, and loyalty. I now look at it as a blessing that we parted ways before I said "I Do" to a man who could have had the power to destroy me. In the meantime, I continue to have faith that my "knight in shining armor" will find me and without hesitation, I will say "Yes" and "I Do".

There were four guiding principles I followed as I worked through heartbreak to restore my sense of confidence and self-worth: Find your peace; forgiveness is for yourself and no one else; and do not let anyone trample on your confidence; and maintain a positive perspective.

Your peace comes by staying true to yourself and values. Trusting yourself to walk away before you let someone else's actions take you out of character and into harm's way.

When we walk in unforgiveness, we remain imprisoned to our previous experiences. Refuse to be locked in prisons within prisons. Forgiveness sets you free to live, love and be whole again.

Your confidence is directly linked to how you perceive yourself, so view yourself as worthy and as a priceless gem.

Maintaining a positive perspective was also vital in conquering this part of my life. Had I not chosen to learn and grow from these experiences, I could be a bitter, man-hating woman spouting toxicity everywhere that my feet tread. Being a pillar of strength for others who cannot yet see that on the other side of their heartbreak they can find and restore their self-worth. Be courageous and know that there is no heartbreak so great that you cannot be healed from over time.

My four guiding principles in this series of tumultuous heartbreaks: **Confidence, Forgiveness, Peace, and Positivity.**

Chapter Three: Reflection Exercise

Guiding principles: Confidence, Forgiveness, Peace, Positivity.

Understanding your worth is one of the most critical things everyone should do to ensure that you quickly recognize those who do not see it and remove yourself from the situation. This pertains to any type of relationship, friendship, romantic relationship, job, etc. Don't let the heartbreak(s) be the discovery point of your worth. For this two-part exercise pick one relationship area to focus on, know that this will require you to be honest with yourself to get the most out of it.

Part 1: Take a moment to write down your top 5 strengths and your 5 areas of opportunity then ask yourself this series of questions:

- When I interact with people for the first time do they see my strengths or my areas of opportunity first?
- What type of mark do I want to leave on the world?
- How do I define my worth?
- If I was on the market for a new friendship and/or relationship, would I choose me? Why or why not?

Part 2: Take a piece of paper and draw 2 vertical lines so that the paper is separated into 3 columns. At the top of the first column write "Must have in a relationship." For the second column, write "Nice to have in a relationship," and the third column becomes "Won't accept in any relationship."

Now take the next 20-30 mins to fill out each column.

After completing part 1 and 2 above, take a moment and reflect on what you have written. What have you learned about yourself by doing this exercise? There is power in the pen!

Now that you have articulated your worth and you have clarified what you need from relationships, let this be a guidepost on how you build and manage relationships moving forward. Set boundaries and do not accept anything less than what you are worth. Spend the next several weeks doing this same exercise for every relationship area (love, friendship, family, coworker).

CHAPTER FOUR
THE SHACKLES OF POVERTY STILL REMAIN...

My early life felt "normal" for the most part. It was difficult for me to imagine that there was a greater frontier to traverse on the outside of "The Meadows."

The Meadows in 90's was a poverty-stricken neighborhood on the north side of Milwaukee, Wisconsin. Most of the families living in this community are single parents with multiple children.

When I was a girl, it was not uncommon to see a single mother of three working a minimum wage job and receiving both food stamps and rental assistance. In this community, you learned how to make a little go a long way. In this community, someone making $40,000 a year is seen as a rich person.

I did not realize until after I left The Meadows, that $40,000 a year cannot afford you the lifestyle to purchase a home, have children, travel, pay for your education and save money for your future endeavors. This stark reality left me puzzled. Unfortunately, what I realized having to utilize government benefits myself after having my children in college was that the system is not set up for you to thrive or even rise. A person must be intentional about how they navigate welfare benefits to break through one chain of poverty. There are multiple chains of poverty and when you break through one chain, there are several more that still shackle you. One of the most challenging chains to break through is the *mindset of poverty.*

I have witnessed the mindset of poverty from the community that I came from, including family members that I still see imprisoned by the deadly disease of poverty. Lack, greed, desperation, materialism, counter-productive engagements, complaining, and hate draw people to remain in this place of stagnancy. Lack: the state of being without or not having enough of something.

I can vividly remember when my mother, younger sister, and I lived in the back room of a bar for a few months. Although my mother was doing the best that she could to survive and take care of her two kids in her home then, she came upon hard times. The father of her last child owned the bar and was a very kind man. Although I was not his biological child, I never felt that way when he was around. If he bought my little sister some clothes, he bought me some too; if he gave her money, he gave me some, too.

The size of the bedroom was 10x10 feet, enough room to have two couches, a rectangular sized end table, a small tv stand and a 40' television. There were two thick black curtains that served as a make-shift door that separated the room from the bar. Darkness smothered the room, allowing just a little peak of dim lights along the vertical sides of the curtains. The top 10 1998 R&B hits playing from the stereo system in the bar area echoed in the room. I can still recite all the words from Deborah Cox's hit that really put her on the map, "Nobody's supposed to be here." That song title was a metaphor for my life during that time. "Nobody's supposed to be staying in a bar as their primary residence."

My mom made my sleeping area as comfortable as possible by layering the couch with multiple blankets and stacking the pillows on top of one another. Tucked completely in where everything below my chin was submersed in the layered blankets. As I lay there, I could not help but allow my thoughts to wander away to the times when life was more normal. My mother and younger sister slept on the couch that had a pull-out bed. Like my setup with layered blankets, this was also replicated on the pull-out bed where the mattress was slightly thicker than a down comforter.

On a good night, I would drift off to sleep around 11:30pm, the bar during the week closed earlier than it does on the weekend so only the "regulars" would come and spend hours in the bar on a Tuesday or Wednesday night. You could always catch the stench so acutely just past the curtains that separated the room from the bar. It was a combination of burned-out cigarettes and Davidoff Cool

Water cologne. The audience tended to be women and men in their late 50's to early 60's. I guess they used the bar to escape the woes of their daily lives.

The name of the bar was "The Wright Spot," playing off the street name on which it was located. It was positioned on the corner of the block, which was considered a high crime area. If you roamed this area any time after sunset, you would not want to travel alone and you would always watch your back. There were very few concerns that things would go astray in the bar, as the owner had a lot of clout in the neighborhood. Mr. Wright contributed to the community in many ways, including providing jobs for those who got caught up in the justice system, but still needed to provide for their families. Lack inundated this community. Many wondered where their next meal was coming from and if they would have enough money to cover their next bill. Experiencing lack was very real for this community.

From my experiences, I witnessed this lack breeding greed and desperation. In my community, The Meadows, people were willing to do anything to obtain what they needed because of this constant lack. This included selling drugs and the mindset that your body is a means of getting resources. Both of these activities were a fast way to obtain money, and the consequences were not even considered. All that mattered was the fact that the lack was seemingly resolved, at least temporarily.

I have personally witnessed people getting caught up in the drug game and losing their lives, losing all of the money they obtained, and ultimately their freedom. Greed and desperation contribute to blurred judgement. Although it may have felt like the person was taking steps forward to rid themselves of the lack, they were really taking leaps backwards. There are very few that enter the drug game and come out unscathed. All it takes is that one moment to get caught either by the police or someone else in the game who feels like you are taking money from their territory. You rarely hear of people who entered the game, capped the amount of money they wanted to make before leaving, and then followed through with their exit. Greed and desperation engulf them, and the potential consequence seems insignificant compared to the potential gain one could experience.

With access to more money than people have ever seen in their lives, the next thing that I witnessed was materialism being born. The fancy cars, designer clothes, blinged out jewelry, exquisite furniture, and expensive shoes – all obtained from drug money. The perception of having these materialistic things carried weight in the community. You were considered part of an elite society. In most cases, these materialistic things only lasted a short while before law enforcement would step onto the scene and take everything that you had risked so much for, including your life, dignity, and family.

After dwelling in the materialistic hemisphere for so long, there is then a door opened for its cousin I call counter-productive engagements. When you appear as if you have "arrived," arrived at a place of perceived success, there is an attraction to you by people who both admire you and envy you at the same time. Purchasing the most fashionable clothes, shoes, cars and jewelry. You are constantly having to reassess a person's motives: is this a genuine interaction or is this a plot to get something from me? You quickly find out who your true friends are. Along with fake friends showing up to get something, there are invitations to places where you are intended to spend money or engage with more foolishness on another level. Counterproductive engagements are intended to keep you down – to keep you stagnant. Those around you who do not have your best interests in mind do not want you to go further or have more than them. It is the crabs in the barrel mentality. As you climb up, there are many trying to pull you right back down. For those who do choose to participate in those engagements, they are often awakened to the reality of the detriment that this causes to a life.

For those strong enough to resist or step away from counterproductive engagements, right next door you meet the other cousin complacency. Now complacency is a very dangerous place because you become so focused on where you currently are that you lose your sense of reality. Becoming so comfortable with the current situation that the vision and the ambition for the future situation becomes blurred, minimizing forward movement in the positive direction. To stagnate, lacking forward movement, eventually pulls you backwards. In this case pulling someone backwards in the hood is an oxymoron, how much further backwards can you go than you already are when you're caught up in this materialistic bubble.

And even if you are one of the "fortunate" ones to escape from this environment, who comes out unscathed from being entangled in the drug scene or held by materialistic bondage, the shackles of poverty remain. Growing up in an environment where lack was a norm, common place, helped shape the way that I viewed the world and engaged with money. Early on, I knew that if I wanted to get an education it would require me to take out student loans. I was willing to do almost anything that would enable me to give my future children a different type of life. A life where they would not experience lack; where they wouldn't have to be placed in situations where they felt like they had to choose between getting an education or working to contribute financially to my household. A well-traveled life, so they never would be afraid of learning outside of the environment that they were born in or be afraid to unapologetically pursue their dreams.

This aspiration was the very thing that carried me through from the moment that I found out I was pregnant with my twins to this very moment. Even when all of my children are adults, this aspiration will carry on to my great, great grandchildren's children. I do not think we always realize the power and authority that we have to break generational stigmas and mindsets and shape our futures in a positive way. We can either become a product of our environment or a champion of helping people break free from the bondage of our past environments.

Don't get me wrong, this is not an easy feat. It takes determination, a purpose-driven mindset, and an ability to keep a positive perspective – to envision your way out of your environment or situation. Especially when times get hard or when you begin to see the residue from the battles that you thought were previously conquered.

When I left home for college, I thought that was going to be the last time that I had to experience living off government assistance. Boy was I wrong! Living from grants offered to me based on my low income and socioeconomic status coming from poverty and student loans, things immediately got challenging when I found out that I was pregnant with twins. I could not afford to work a job where I would have a consistent flow of money or great health insurance while continuing to pursue my Engineering degree. This put me in a situation where I needed government assistance to help fill the gap. When I left for college, I thought that I had broken the chains of poverty, but that was just an illusion. I entered parenthood as a young mom of 22 years old, filled with so much hope and tenacity around fulfilling my future goals and recommitted to ensuring my children experienced a different childhood environment than I had.

It was super empowering to accept my first engineering job offer and to know that I was back on track with breaking the chains of poverty. The income bracket immediately disqualified me from obtaining any government assistance. My children now had access to great health insurance, and I could financially provide for my children without burden or embarrassment.

I was extremely fortunate to break free from a level of poverty. I could have easily taken advantage of government assistance as a hinderance or crutch (instead of taking the engineering job or meaning used more of it than you needed?) versus as a steppingstone, keeping me from reaching my full potential. Growing up in my community, I had thought of $40,000 a year as a lot of money. It took me landing my first engineering job, which paid $110,000 plus salary and realizing that the more money you make, the more taxes you pay. Then add on taking care of children, maintaining a household, saving, student loan repayment, traveling, and nights of entertainment with friends and that money dwindles fast.

Looking back at my childhood, I have a greater appreciation of how my mother was able to take care of four children, bringing in about half of what I made. Although we did not have a lot, it never felt like we had less than anyone else. As I began to interact with people who were raised in different environments and came from very different socio-economic backgrounds, I only then realized the things I didn't have as they shared their stories of childhood. I was the first and only person in my family to pursue an Engineering degree. I did not have a trust fund or family wealth. My mother did not have money saved for me to attend college, and my grandparents on mom's side did not have land that they could leave to their descendants or an inheritance that would be split among their heirs. Compared to many of my peers who did not have the additional weight of student loan debt or having to pay the "Black tax", I started out in Corporate America with a deficiency.

The 'Black tax' refers to the additional burden that can come with being the first, only, or one in a few in your family to break barriers and enter arenas that may have never been tapped in previous generations due to systemic racism and slavery. Immediate family and extended family are now depending on you. If there is a need, you are the first to be asked because "you made it." The student loan debt becomes invisible because all that they can see is the "success" you have obtained. Being the person who was able to achieve their dreams, you are often guilty because you know first-hand what it feels like to be in the middle of the struggle. You sacrifice building your wealth for the future to help your loved ones in the present. This is also why it is so important to have equity in the workplace. Not being compensated equitably and fairly has a disproportionate impact on me, my children, my friends and family, and my community because they depend on me to show up.

I still have student loan debt, but I have gotten a lot better with balancing supporting my family and friends and securing for my future. Although this chain of poverty is still connected to me, I have made a commitment that this will not be a chain to which my children will be bound. They will pursue their future endeavors graduating high school without the stress of having excessive financial burdens to worry about. My sacrifice will pay dividends for their futures and that is enough for me.

The trials and tribulations of coming from poverty have taught me a lot and I am grateful for the life lessons. I had to learn how to survive and thrive with minimum financial means, causing me to be highly creative in my endeavors. I learned how to stretch what little I had, and to celebrate the small victories, continuing to push despite how daunting my immediate circumstances may have appeared. The premise for these learnings goes back to my guiding principle threaded in each chapter of this book— the ability to maintain a positive perspective Although the shackles of poverty remain for me today including extensive student loan debt, lack of owning real estate and residual investments, they will not remain forever.

I have a responsibility and opportunity to break those chains so that my children won't have to deal with that same bondage as they embark on their adulthood journeys.

Chapter Four: Reflection Exercise

Guiding principles: Determination, Purpose-Driven, Positivity.

Imagine what it would feel like to run in quicksand. Perspective matters. Take about 20 minutes to reflect on those times in your life when you may have felt stuck, what were some of the key actions that you had to take to break free. If you say, "there are areas in my life where I'm feeling really stuck and have no clue on where to start to break free." I want you to close your eyes, clear your mind by counting backwards from the number 30. Now imagine what did it felt like before you got to this place of being stuck and write down everything that comes to mind. Once you finish that, I know what you to write a list that reflects what you think led to you being stuck in the first place. Lastly, has a symbolism of breaking free I want you to verbally Denounce the items that brought you to that place of being stuck and proclaim the feelings you felt before you became stuck.

❖ **Denounce:** I am no longer in agreement with the negative impacts that being stuck have had on my life.
o The hurt that I may have caused myself and/or others does not have to hinder me from apologizing, writing my wrongs and being intentional about contributing to the lives of others in a positive way
❖ **Proclaim:** I decree that I am from everything that has held me in bondage and has hindered me from reaching my full potential.
o I will not allow the broken parts of my past creep into my future and minimize the view that I have of myself or my ability to love myself and others unconditionally.

CHAPTER FIVE
COVID CAME, BUT WE CONQUERED

I remember March of 2020 so vividly, as there were a series of monumental events that happened during that month. But let's go backwards in time for a moment and talk about the 3 months leading up to March of 2020. There was a lot of anticipation leading up to New Years Eve of 2019 for me. This year was expected to be different than any other year. "2020 represents 20/20 vision, where things will become perfectly aligned in your life."

I prepared for embarking on the big things in store for me. My best friend and I planned a trip in January to California. This was a dream of hers since she was a little girl that we were about to make come true. At this point she was living in Indiana, and I was living in Washington State. We had the absolute time of our lives! We saw all the touristy attractions: Hollywood Boulevard, Madam Tussaud's Wax Museum, Ripley's Believe It or Not, Santa Monica Pier and the Nipsey Hussle Memorial, just to name a few. Less than a week a week after being home on Jan 26th, the US was shaken by the plane crash in the California area that took the lives of Kobe Bryant, his daughter, and several other people on the aircraft that were heading back from a basketball game that the girls had just played. This was utterly painful for so many; 2020 had landed a bomb that none of us had expected.

The day we returned home on January 20, 2020, was the day that the CDC confirmed its first case of Covid-19. What a way to end our girls' trip with news about a virus that was deemed to have the potential to become a pandemic and impact the lives of so many across the world. At that time, we had no idea about how devastating this journey would be.

Uncertainty appeared every way that you turned; a pandemic of this magnitude had never occurred in many people's lifetimes. When you turned on the news, all you saw was the death total and rising Covid cases around the world. People were being advised to stay in their homes and wear personal protective equipment like masks and gloves. Uncertainty, unexpectedly in the blink of an eye, moved across the world. Uncertainty quickly became layered with fear, pain, grief, disappointment, sorrow, anger, impatience, fatigue (mental, physical, emotional, and financial), with continued uncertainty of what was to come the next day.

The compounded effect of this uncertainty sandwich has had a lasting effect on everyone for the last two and a half years and will continue to have effects for decades to come. There were people who lost their entire immediate family to this deadly virus. The type of pain that those individuals experienced is unimaginable. Many did not even have the opportunity to say their final goodbyes because of restrictions set in order to minimize spread of the virus. This era has left permanent scar on the hearts of so many and there are some wounds that time will not completely heal...There is but a moment between "certainty" and "un-certainty."

In the midst of the pain and uncertainty that the world was experiencing as the pandemic claimed the lives of millions of people, the Black community within the US was experiencing a man-made pandemic. The use of excessive force by law enforcement against Black men and boys. The entire world watched in agony the video of George Floyd being murdered under a police officer's knee placed on his neck, suffocating him for no just cause. Watching this grown man struggle to breathe as he called out for his deceased mother right before taking his last breath was heart-wrenching. There were protests in the streets of US cities and cities abroad for months consisting of people from all backgrounds and nationalities.

This was an enlightening moment for all, showing the stark reality that racism was still real in the United States of America. Immediately corporations began to put statements in the media denouncing the brutal act of this Black man killed by a police officer. They also professed their commitment to support their Black employees and ensure they explore any areas within their company that could be perceived as racist. The Black Lives Matter movement took off like a lightning bolt at this moment in history. It is sad because there have been so many Black men, women and children who have lost their lives at the hands of a police officer using excessive force. The George Floyd moment opened the infected wound that the Black community had been trying to heal and make sense of for years. Was justice eventually served? Somewhat. The officer who performed the act was convicted, but the officers who stood by and just watched a fellow officer kill an innocent Black man were not. Was that the last excessive act on the Black community? Absolutely not. This is still a work in progress and requires the world to be empathic and stand up when injustice is present, especially those in positions of privilege, power, and decision-making circles.

Top companies across the United States did exactly that, used their power and privilege to decry the acts of racism. This included defunding projects that may have extremist views when it comes to race. Companies internally sent emails to the Black community and broader community providing support to the employees and re-affirming their stance that everyone, no matter their background, is valued. The company where I was working during that time immediately put time on everyone's calendar to have "Inclusive Dialogues," providing space for the Black community to feel heard, articulate disappointment, and share the emotional strain caused by watching this unfold on the television screen. Plenty others and I were baffling with the idea that George Floyd could have easily been our father, brother, son, uncle, friend, or cousin, causing us not to feel safe and feeling the need to have 'that talk' with our family members on how to engage with law enforcement: "If you are in the car, immediately put your hands on the steering wheel. Before they arrive at your window, have your license and registration placed in your hand as your hands rest on the steering wheel. Do not make any sudden moves, announce your moves but get permission before doing so. The goal is for you to return home with no harm to yourself!"

There was emphasis on 'Mental Health' like never before as companies allocated additional days off to employees allowing them the autonomy to take time as they needed to process through the state of chaos the world was in. Taking my first mental health day was extremely liberating—pretty amazing to dedicate time to take care of your mental well-being. I took that day to unpack my thoughts and assess what I needed in my day-to-day life to not become bogged down with stress or worry. I minimized the amount of news I consumed through television and social media outlets. I made time and space to capture my thoughts with journaling. I provided a safe space for my teenage boys to articulate their opinions on the current state of the world and how this informs how they navigate it. Finally, I took time to re-evaluate my life to date; Am I happy? Are there things that I can do differently? What do I want my future to look like? Am I walking in Purpose?

My mental health day turned into a mental health movement for me. I was so accustomed to carrying burdens, hardships, and disappointments, and still pushing to conquer life, that I was not giving myself permission to truly feel, as if making time to 'feel' minimized my journey or was not warranted. It was this big subconscious lie that I never knew that I was telling myself. To truly embrace this movement that I was thrusted into required me to first feel (be in the moment), to be honest with myself and to forgive myself for all the times that I prioritized everything but my own well-being. Up until this point in my life, I had dealt with so many moments of uncertainty but not until Covid did I have to dwell in it. Ironically, staying in that place of uncertainty set my future; with faith, love, and compassion I am now able to overcome my many moments of uncertainty.

In March of 2020, I made the decision to move in 15 months to the only place within the US that I physically felt purpose the moment my feet touched the ground upon my first visit. There was almost a 10-year gap between me feeling purpose and taking the physical step to align in purpose. This was also the same month that I decided to leave my job in a stable industry at the beginning of the pandemic to work in a very unstable industry. Although about 90% of my circle may have thought that I was crazy, 8% kept their silence and 2% said anything at all. I was not moved by the thoughts or opinions, and I knew without the shadow of a doubt that it was the right thing for me to do. I had no clue at that moment, that me walking away from that job was my first step into walking towards my purpose.

Before I made a physical move out of state, there was a physical move that I had to do within the state. There was certainty in my decision, as I knew deep down in my heart that it was the right thing to leave. The seven months almost to the date of losing my father and the day of my big move were heart-wrenching and liberating at the same time. Closing on chapter of my life in Washington where my dad lived for almost 20 years and where I met him for the first time, and starting a chapter symbolizing me physically taking a step into "purpose". I created a plan to ensure a smooth transition, with this new chapter. I gathered details pertaining to the top three cities that I would move to, the number of bedrooms my house would need, the diversity within the neighborhood, and the school rating for my boys' high school. Some days were better than others; either I spent most of day pondering on the sadness that I had associated with my father and his passing, or I spent time researching my soon-to-be new residence.

During this time, the boys expressed their excitement about starting our new chapter. They were looking forward to being in a state that had more sun and less rain, the new friends they would meet after starting high school and living in a bigger home. Knowing that the boys agreed with this move made things easier for me. Had they shown disappointment or hesitation, it may have impacted the timing in which I made the move. At the forefront of my mind when I made major life changes, was always to minimize as much friction as possible for my children and cause the least amount of disruption possible. We planned to make the move right after their eighth grade graduation, allowing a few months to acclimate to a new area before their freshman year would begin.

Of course, with every big decision that you make in life there are always challenges waiting right around the corner. In this case, the first incident started in March of 2021 when one of the twins woke up and one of his feet was swollen like a balloon. Given that there was no known injury that provoked the swelling, I was advised by his doctor to take him into the ER. There was certainly some anxiety associated with this trip to the ER, as the number of Covid patients in the hospital was still very high. We arrived at the hospital with our standard gear, and immediately after entering we were prompted to sit on one side or the other. "If you are experiencing Covid symptoms, sit in the lobby to your right, no symptoms sit in the lobby on your left." Shortly after checking in the nurses did the standard temperature and vitals check, then escorted him back to be evaluated. After a physical exam, X-rays, and an ultrasound of his right leg, the doctors did not have an explanation on what was causing the swelling. We were told to ice and elevate his foot, take Tylenol for any pain, and return if the symptoms worsened. Over the next few days, there was a very slight difference in the swelling, but my son no longer complained of any pain. I thought that the coast was clear and that the swelling would go away completely soon.

Now let's fast forward to May 1st of 2021. I had just finished taking a trip from visiting my best friend for her book signing. Before taking my flight back to Seattle, I was extremely tired but did not think much of it as it was a long weekend. A few days after being home, I knew something was not right as I began to get sicker and sicker by the hour, it seemed. My best friend was also experiencing some of the same symptoms by this point and we knew it was time for a Covid test. Ironically, the tests came back negative and no one else in either of our households was experiencing any symptoms. By day six, I felt like I was hit by a ton of bricks and knew on the inside that I had Covid. With the little strength that I had by this point, I went to the drive-through testing center and within two hours I had tested positive for Covid. There was a slight relief in simply knowing the battle that I was up against and the fact that the only symptom that I had not experienced was shortness of breath. I had fever, chills, cough, fatigue, body aches, headache, loss of taste/smell, sore throat, congestion, and nausea. I also had no desire to eat or drink anything. My doctor stated most people started feeling better by day fourteen and suggested that I go to the ER if breathing issues occurred. I spent the next 7-8 days enduring as much as I could. Still logging into work and taking medicine and naps when needed. Everything came to a head on day fourteen. I woke up and had numbness from my left shoulder down my entire right side. Overwhelmed with the fear of me potentially having a heart attack, I begin to have a panic attack. I immediately contacted my doctor and was advised to go to the ER. This was my second trip to the ER within 60 days, this time for myself.

I arrived at the hospital and followed the same prompts that were given when I took my son a few weeks earlier, this time going to the lobby on my right instead of the left. All my initial vitals appeared normal but given the numbness and burning sensation I was having the doctor ordered an EKG. The EKG came back normal as well, so my doctor decided to do some research as I was the first patient, he had seen experiencing these additional symptoms. After about 45 minutes in the room, the doctor returns and says, "After doing some additional research, it looks like you fall into the two-percent bucket of people who have neurological issues associated with Covid." In shock, I had so many questions to which the doctor did not have answers. Leave it to me to have yet another anomaly come up in my life. My journey has been filled with anomalies, so I should not have been too surprised.

At this time, I was officially on day fourteen where my symptoms were supposed to start getting better but in my case my symptoms were getting worse and in a rare way. The standard Covid symptoms diminished but the neurological symptoms intensified. In addition to the numbness and burning sensation, I experienced extreme fatigue, migraines, even short-term and long-term memory loss. This made my Covid journey extremely frightening, not knowing what the future would hold and whether I would ever return to my "normal."

With all the challenges I was facing, this still was not enough for me to take time off work. I was so worried about not being able to complete my work, end of year pressures, and not wanting to let my team down. At this moment, I was choosing everything but me. Well, at least until about day eighteen of my Covid journey when I had to take my son back to the ER for the second time in 60 days. He complained of his symptoms worsening on his right side, instead of just feeling it in his foot, he was now experiencing pain in his thigh. All bets were off pertaining to everything around me when I got the news that my son had blood clots in his thigh that were undetected when we took the ER trip in March.

Knowing this information, I immediately sent my manager at that time a text message stating that I would be taking leave as she had suggested I do two weeks prior. It took my son having this life-threatening event for me to choose me. There was never a question about me prioritizing my children over anything, but I could not understand why I did not have that same passion to look after myself. I was still extremely sick but was willing to push for things that really did not matter in the grand scheme. My decision to take short-term leave was me committing myself to take care of my son and my own well-being. Looking back, I still cannot believe that it took this series of events to prioritize my physical well-being.

I mentioned at the beginning of this chapter that I understood the importance of taking care of my mental well-being, but somewhere in that equation I did not include my physical well-being. From that experience I have learned the importance of your "total well-being" - physical, spiritual, mental, and emotional. I have made a personal commitment not to compromise any area of my "total well-being." What I also realized is that making that type of commitment to my well-being was me setting boundaries for my life and acknowledging my 'worth'.

> **"I am worthy of good health, a sound mind, and taking time away from work when needed and unapologetically."**

I do not want to leave you all in suspense of my son and his progress as I close out this chapter, so here is the update. I extended my leave from work to 12 weeks to dedicate undivided attention to my son and his health. It took about 9 months for my neurological symptoms to significantly dissipate. Now that it is now a little over a year past my Covid encounter, I am almost 100 percent back to Normal. For my son, it took an entire year to mitigate the blood clots and swelling after a series of blood thinner injections and oral medication. Although this impacted his entire freshman year, he's excited about the start of his upcoming sophomore year.

Chapter Five: Reflection Exercise

Guiding principles: Faith, Sacrifice, Compassion, Love, Positivity.

Have you given yourself space and time to evolve into the person that you are meant to be? If Covid hadn't done anything else, it turned the world upside down. The fear, loss, scarcity, lack of hope and uncertainty left marks on our lives that we never expected. If you are reading this book, you made it through one of the most tumultuous times in the last few centuries and that is a moment to celebrate all by itself!

Take the next 30-45 mins and journal about all the things that you are grateful for. Include what you learned about yourself while going through the Covid era and how you plan on optimizing your learnings in your future.

CHAPTER SIX
ALIGNING WITH PURPOSE

June 26th, 2021 was the big day! The day that I took the physical step to get aligned with purpose for this stage in my life. 15 months of planning was finally paying off. Although uncertain about several aspects, I was certain in the depths of my being, making the move to a state that symbolized me physically stepping/aligning with my purpose was the right thing to do.

The certainty came from the euphoric experience I had when my feet first touched the soil of the 'state' several years prior. When my feet touched the ground, I physically felt 'purpose.' In that moment there were connections, conviction, and an overwhelming sense of completion.

Purpose: the reason for which something was created and/or exists. The 'why' behind the navigation and the understanding of the impact you are called to make on the world. Discovering purpose requires intentionality and focus, exploring those areas of your life where there is a sense of incompletion. It is a marathon and not a sprint when on a quest to discover and walk in purpose. It is also personal. Although you may have others walk alongside you on the journey, no one can walk on your behalf. Your purpose' is uniquely designed, and tailor made for you.

My purpose (why I exist) and mission statement (what I do and for whom) are intertwined, "To empower everyone that I encounter to become the best version of themselves and discover purpose." Over time, additional levels of depth' is added to my purpose positioning me to anchoring my why' to everything that I do, from setting goals to obtaining them. For this stage of my life aligning with my purpose meant me taking the intentional steps of becoming the best version of myself in a State where I felt like it was conducive for me to grow and rediscover the things that truly make my heart smile. Prior to this point, I spent three and a half years living in a State where I felt like I was trapped in a hamster wheel. Repetitive routine that consisted of me going to work, taking care of the twins, providing counsel to others then rinse and repeat. Some may argue that I was living in my purpose in that moment and agree that it was true to a certain extent. I was invested into all of my respective responsivities and contributing to society in a why that was allowing me to empower everyone that I encountered to become the best version of themselves, but yet I still felt like something was missing. When my feet' touched the ground in the new state there was a spark reignited that obliterated the feeling of something' missing that quite honestly, I didn't share with many people.

Me not sharing had everything to do with me not wanting

to be judged or discouraged from pursuing a path that felt right to me. I made the decision to move at the beginning of the Covid pandemic, where people were cautioned to not leave their homes expect for necessity purposes and I made the bold declaration about moving to another state. There was no one else in my direct circle who were considering a similar decision, I was going against the grain. I've learned that pursuing purpose may require you to make bold decisions and require you to sit in that decision alone. Holding this decision close to my chest empowered me to fall into the pitfall that I dwelt in many times, people pleasing.

There were several times I felt that I had to get validation from people around me, before taking that physical step into purpose. As I know all too well, resisting the path that people-pleasing can take you on is no easy feat. It can lead to you taking off in a direction where you do not know where you are heading and do not recognize the person that you are becoming along the way.

Interpreting the thoughts, ideals, limitations, and fears of others as part of your own purpose is difficult to recognize and fight against.

As I mentioned earlier, purpose is personal, and it is directly connected to *your* "why"—not someone else's. People-pleasing can take you down a dangerous spiral, where your why and your worth feel like your own but are really controlled and shaped by someone else. I remember the bondage that I felt when I was entangled in being a people-pleaser. Focusing more on other people's needs and desires while neglecting my own. Becoming a robot, and in some cases quite frankly a doormat, as I stray further away from my own purpose. My thoughts became other people's thoughts of me, as a result creating an unhealthy relationship with myself and others.

Let's spend time on the "creating an unhealthy relationship with myself" statement for a moment. If I look at myself in the mirror and all I see looking back at me are the perceptions that others have about me, it will make it extremely hard to truly know and love myself. It can be especially harmful when those perceptions make me feel like I could never measure up or make me feel like I am a failure because I am not fulfilling someone else's expectations. It is nearly impossible for someone to discover purpose without self-love. The purpose journey requires you to be honest with yourself, and to believe that your flaws and your strengths make you the unique 'you' that the world needs. It is of utmost importance to trust yourself and understand that not everyone will agree with every decision you make. That is okay if it feels true to you and is not causing harm to anyone else.

"If I do not live up to their expectation of me, will they still love me or accept me?"

There was an internal power and freedom that I was able to tap into after having this revelation. When you are not bound by the perceptions of others, you actually have the time and energy to double down on yourself, discovering who you really are and deciding how you want to show up in the world. Through this discovery process you find authenticity. I would be lying if I said that this process of breaking through to purpose was not heart wrenching for me. Many times, I could not see past the possibility of losing a relationship that I thought I really wanted. My inner monologue was doubting myself, not the intentions of others who wished to control me.

There is a line in a song by one of my favorite artists Fantasia that states "Sometimes you have to lose to win again." I absolutely love these words because there is so much truth in them. Along your journey of purpose, you must be okay with letting people go who are not committed to loving you selflessly and without judgment as you discover and become the real you.

I remember that plane ride to the new state like it was yesterday. As I gazed out the window and thought to myself "I really don't know what the details of this physical stop will look like but I'm trusting that all of the pieces will fall together, as this decision feels true to me." Sometimes we get so caught up in not knowing exactly how our decisions will play out that we become immobilized by fear. Fear is another thing that will keep us from embarking on the purpose journey, fear of the unknown.

When the plane landed, I was overwhelmed with joy and excitement! I chose me and was not moved by the opinions that people had about how my new home could impact my life or career. I spent the first 60 days taking in all the moments and setting my intentions on what I wanted this chapter of my life to look like. Exploring the city, meeting people in my neighborhood, and intentionally participating in cultural activities that made my heart smile - a heart I had abandoned the previous three and a half years of my life. Just these acts alone made me feel closer to defining 'purpose' for this new life stage. It caused me to reflect on the things that really feed my soul - learning and experiencing new things, creating and experiencing a sense of community, cultural engagements, and being intentional about contributing to society in a positive way. Finding the things that make your heart smile takes you another step forward.

> *Your purpose is multi-facet and is not static but it continues to evolve as you navigate life, we should give ourselves permission and space to become.*

As I mentioned earlier, this is a marathon and not a sprint. At this stage of my life, taking the time to rediscover what makes my heart smile was exactly what I needed to be aligned with purpose.

Here were the steps that I took to discover Purpose:

- Created space to remove all distractions and sit quietly with myself, the noise from the opinions of others around you as the power to cloud your discovery.
- Reflected on my life journey to-date, dissecting the highlights and the lowlights while identifying the common threads in those moments. Those common threads often linked to the things that I

am really passionate about. I believe that your
passions are closely connected to your purpose.

- Created my intertwined mission statement that I
use as a compass for how I navigate the world and
engage with others. This gives me an anchor point
for holding myself accountable to living in Purpose.

Holding myself accountable for staying true to my Purpose
consists of having a regular routine of self-reflection.
Pondering and meditating on my mission statement and
being honest about whether I am living up to it and course-
correcting when I am not. Honesty is one of the greatest
gifts that we can give to ourselves when staying true to
living in purpose. I would be lying if I say that I always "get
it right", I am not perfect and no one else either. In those
moments I acknowledge where I fell short, forgive myself
and change my behavior when showing up the next time.

When I'm out of alignment with purpose the changes
within myself and are sometimes subtle, if I am not
intentional about self-reflecting and can be missed until I
feel the compound effects of being out of alignment for
too long. It shows up in my attitude, perspective on life
situations, the effort that I put into my responsibilities,
motivation or lack thereof and my interactions that I have
with others.

When we align with purpose, we exude a light that
encourages others to align with theirs.

Chapter Six: Reflection Exercise

Guiding principle: Faith, Determination, Intentionality, Positivity.

Image that you have reached the place of euphoria (all things perfect in your eyes), take about 15 mins to jot down what that place looks, smells and feels like. What are the elements that you love most about that place and why? How will you know that you have arrived at that place? What are actions that you can take in your life now that can give you similar satisfaction?

Spend some time over the next 30 days dissecting the elements you love most about 'your' place of euphoria, through this experience you'll get a step closer to discovering your purpose. This isn't meant to be an easy purpose finder experience as it takes years to discover 'purpose', but a tool that can be used as you go on an intentional purpose discovery journey. Here is my purpose summed up into one sentence, "To encourage everyone that I encounter to become the best version of themselves and to discover purpose". I know first-hand the power that you tap into when aligning to purpose. When you walk in purpose everything around you responds, there is an energy that you exude, and others are attracted to that.

CHAPTER SEVEN
LET LOVE BE YOUR SUPERPOWER

Unconditional Love (1 Corinthians 13) is patient, love is kind, love is long suffering, love is selfless, love is not prideful, love does not envy, love still remains even when it is not reciprocated in the manner that you desire, love does not keep count of any wrongdoings (this one is by far the HARDEST to practice), and love never fails as it is for eternity.

I approach every encounter with my heart first, which has manifested great joy and great pain throughout my life. I have been on both sides of the fence many times, having my heart shredded to pieces and having my heart mended whole again with little to no residue from the previous assault. It was not easy to endure, but those experiences helped shape me into the person I am today. I have empathy for the world as everyone is on their individual journeys through life. The journey is not a sprint, it is a cross-country run requiring you to evaluate your thoughts, actions and take accountability when you discover moments where you did not show up as love. I believe that love is the cure to almost everything that's plaguing society; everything from racism and violence to the lack of respect for humanity and our planet.

My love walk has truly been the thing that has set me apart. It has served as both a blessing and a curse at times. I have found that most people have never experienced the type of love that I exude, and it is often first met with rejection. It is foreign, and just like anything else new that you encounter for the first time, the immediate response my not be overwhelming acceptance.

Let's go back to the beginning for a moment. I was conceived through love, wounded love, but love all the same. My parents loved each other the best way that they knew how based on their own past experiences that left scars on their heart. Both being the first born of their married parents and, interestingly enough, having the same number of children, four. My parents were not married, and I am the only child that the two shared together, the third child for both of them. Given that they separated before finding out that they were pregnant with me, I never witnessed my parents showing up as a family unit. That image only showing up sparsely in my dreams, a white picket fence with both of my parents present' in the home and ready to tend to my needs. Maybe this was the same dream that my parents had about their mothers and fathers; history has a tendency to repeat itself if we do not make a conscious decision to do things differently.

Both of my parents were born in the 1950's, where their lineage began in the south and it was common to marry young. My mother's side is from Mississippi; her parents were about 16 and 18 years old when she was conceived. They did the best that they could but ended up going their separate ways by the time that she was seven years old. I have never heard my mother say that her parents modeled what love should truly look like between spouses. My father's beginnings were remarkably similar; parents being around the same age and parents separating before he turned the age of ten. Since my father was not there when I was younger and our reconnection was short-lived, I never got a chance to ask him about his early childhood. His mother's side is from Illinois and his father's side from Arkansas. All that I have are the stories shared by my grandmother, parting ways from her spouse was the best thing they could do for one another at that time. If you never see love modeled, I believe it impacts how you perceive love and how you extend it.

At that age that my grandparents married, it is hard to tell if you truly know what love is. When I go back to my 18-year-old self, I was extremely naive to what love looked and felt like. As a little girl, I was always very affectionate. I wanted to be hugged, kissed, and told "I love you" as much as possible. The environment that I grew up in was not conducive to receiving the type of love that I desired, often causing me to feel out of place or even inane for having such a desire. I learned how to suppress my emotions very well. From the age that I could form memories, I remember my mother was not the affectionate type. She showed her love through the things that she provided for me. She would go out of her way to make sure that we had gifts for the holidays, even if that meant her spending her last dollar. However, the words or the touch of love did not happen very often. But I cannot fault my mother as she showed love the way she experienced it and the best way she knew how. The older that I got and after being around others who invited me in as extended family, I realized that the way I desired to experience love was not foolish, it was simply different than to what I was accustomed. I found myself being comfortable showing the affectionate side of me through my friendships and my romantic relationships. Giving hugs and saying I love you on a consistent basis became a part of my everyday language.

But I did not receive the full magnitude of love being felt until I gave birth to my twin boys. Now that is a love that I cannot even articulate in words, the epitome of selflessness. I made a commitment to making sure that all the love that I had bottled up inside of me, I would bestow on my boys. All the hugs, kisses, and "I love you" they could ever think about asking for. Through loving them in that manner, I made a conscious decision to extend a similar type of love to anyone that I encountered in hopes of giving people an opportunity to experience unconditional love. The kind of love that I described earlier is pure in its intent and does not seek to gain anything in return by extending it. Now I would be remiss if I said that this love journey has been filled with roses and lilies - it came with some thorns and daggers. What I came to realize is that there are not a lot of people who are accustomed to receiving the love that I was extending to the world. It was often met first with doubt and rejection. Yet another point in my life where I showed up as unique or different, but this time with extending my love to the world.

I have refused to let those difficult moments take me through a cycle of suppressing my desire to receive and give affectionate love. I truly believe that love is one of the greatest gifts that you can give to anybody.

Love has the power to break down walls, alienate biases, heal the heart, heal the world, and create space for people to show up as their whole selves.

Why is this important? We all share a responsibility in contributing to the greater good of society, leading with unconditional love is a sure way of doing that. What I have learned is that when you lead with love and a whole heart, others will extend theirs. This is also when I realized that love was one of my super-powers. It is that special power that when it shows up purely, transforms hearts and minds. Since we can only connect dots looking backwards, I would have never been able to identify my personal mission statement without understanding my super-power. "To empower everyone that I encounter to become the best version of themselves and to discover purpose" - this is all enabled through my superpower.

To arrive at this place of actualization, it took me first going on an exploratory journey to understand who I am and being honest about the areas that I suppressed due to being seen as 'different' in environments I was in. This required me to break free from the "people-pleasing" tendencies I once had.

Secondly, I had to get comfortable with the fact that 'different' does not mean 'bad.' Having differences is what makes the world beautiful, and our unique DNA is a necessary contribution. Thirdly, I had to proactively address the broken areas of my heart. When my feelings are hurt, I no longer ignore them but take time to explore the 'why' and resolve whatever breach may have occurred to my heart. These three steps are not one and done activities but require re-evaluation at different points in your life. The points could correlate with major life events, like starting a new job or starting a new friendship and/or romantic relationship.

When we are not intentional about addressing our heart wounds, we unintentionally cut others with our broken pieces.

Let's make a proclamation daily, "I'm going to be intentional about addressing the wounds of my heart, so that I don't cut others with my broken pieces." Let's say that again and let it really marinate in your soul, "I'm going to be intentional about addressing the wounds of my heart, so that I don't cut others with My broken pieces".

This declaration is a proclamation of Love. What hinders us from giving and receiving love in the manner we were intended has everything to do with the matters of our heart! If everyone on the planet made this commitment, I trust that we would be living in Utopia.

I have learned along this journey that some things are just not meant to be understood by everyone. This has required me to not keep count of wrongdoings, or a tally of how many times I have been hurt. As I mentioned earlier, this is the hardest of all of the attributes of love to practice. This applies to both instances, extending love and receiving love. I have had to apply this logic to all areas of my life to keep my peace and my sanity: Family, Friendships and Romantic Relationships.

In each of these areas I have examples of when I have given "all of me," and in return I have been hurt seemly for no reason. I have realized that everyone is at a different place in there healing journey and their "all of me" effort may look different than yours. You must extend Grace and show empathy, although you may not understand everything at that moment. Sometimes you must love someone from a distance, as they may need space to go on their healing journey alone and to protect your own heart. You must learn how to move forward, despite uncertainty to keep yourself from being in bondage. Knowing that all human beings are flawed and that we will all fall short along life's journey, let's not allow this to keep us from being free and loving generously.

I conducted an exercise where I asked four people who are within my trusted circle three simple questions, their responses were very validating, affirming and heartwarming. With transparency and vulnerability, I have shared their response below. Whenever I need to be re-grounded or reminded of how my superpower impacts the lives of others in a positive way especially when challenging times arise or self-doubt tries to show up on the scene, I reread these responses. Along this journey we will always have our supporters and nay-sayers, we just have to make sure that the voice of our supporters is LOUDER than the nay-sayers.

Three simple questions.

1. How have I shown you love?

2. How has the love I've shown impacted your life in a positive or negative way?

3. Based on this definition of love, what areas do you feel that I have opportunities to grow and where have you seen me excel? "Love is patient, love is kind, love is long suffering, love is selfless, love is not prideful, love does not envy, love still remains even when it's not reciprocated in the manner that you desire, love does not keep count of any wrongdoings and love never fails it's for eternity."

Here are the responses that I received from 4 people in my close circle.

Pooh's Response

How have I shown you love?

When I think about how we met, at a little revival in Indy it was a peculiar experience within itself. I was seeking an encounter from God and had an encounter with an already birthed God given friend and sister. Your heart was open and ready where my heart had been broken from shattered relationships and guarded and skeptical. You showed me love unconditionally despite my brokenness and flawed views. You prayed for me when my heart wasn't quite ready to receive the love I so desperately needed. Your love never failed over the years, and it covered a lot of misunderstandings to say the least. Your love was pure and unyielding and pulled me through the darkest hours.

How has the love I've shown impacted my life in a negative or positive way?

Love is contagious and after a while you will catch its undeniable fruit. The love you have shown has been nothing short of positive. It has helped me embrace the positive healthy friendships and sisterhood I now enjoy. You refined the thought that women don't just wound they can heal love teach and embrace.

Based on the definition of love what areas do you feel I have opportunities to grow and where have you seen me excel?

Based on this definition of love, what areas do you feel that I have opportunities to grow and where have you seen me excel? "Love is patient, love is kind, love is long suffering, love is selfless, love is not prideful, love does not envy, love still remains even when it's not reciprocated in the manner that you desire, love does not keep count of any wrongdoings and love never fails it's for eternity." When it comes to love honestly, I think it's you're gifting. I know that it has been tested truly over the years. My prayer is that you are always abounding in love, being steadfast and immovable. I love you.

Samaj's Response

How have I shown you love?

Tameka(Mom) has shown me Love numerous times. Tameka introduced me to a loving life that I always dreamed of but never really knew was real. When I first met Tameka (mom) in high school there was a 75% chance that I was going to the navy, but she booked me a flight to Seattle, Washington around June of 2019. She showed me everything she does on a daily basis that so happen to be exactly how I dreamed of living my life. Tameka (mom) showed me unforgettable views and helped me face my fear of heights. She introduced me to her loving sons and genuine friends. Tameka even showed me what she does to escape everything.

How has the love I've shown impacted my life in a negative or positive way?

Tameka's Love taught me that there is more to life than just signs, we have to understand the meanings to take along with us on our journeys. So, when I returned home, I began my own new journey with Tameka guiding and rooting for me along the way. I faced a lot of hardships in my journey but there was never once Tameka wasn't there for me when I needed her. She gave me room to fall flat on my face when I was going in the wrong direction. Tameka's love is so unconditional that every lesson I faced I've come back to her with my wisdom and revelations from my battles. Tameka's Love showed me to appreciate everything I endured as a child and to not question it. I have now accepted my past and understand that without the wisdom and strength I gained from those experiences I wouldn't be who I am today. everyone hasn't taken that chance to help me face my fears like she has, Tameka is a conqueror beyond the naked eye's view.

Based on the definition of love what areas do you feel I have opportunities to grow and where have you seen me excel?

Tameka's love has impacted my life positively since the start of us meeting each other. Tameka motivates me to pursue my future and put my best foot forward at all times. In my eyes Tameka has excelled in being patient with me during my ups and downs. My journey is not easy but Tameka doubles down with me and goes all in for me. She's an amazing mother figure to me and I want to thank God, he sent her to be a guiding light in my life.

Denise's Response

How have you shown love?

The dictionary defines showing love as "not a feeling. To love is to feel and act lovingly". Let me begin by saying you have done a marvelous job in showing love. It is an act but there is so much I could add so I have catered my definition of showing love specifically to you. I'm blessed to say that I have experienced firsthand love from you

Sunlight and yes, I call her Sunlight and she calls me Sunshine. Sunlight is the daughter I never had but is selfless beyond measure. What does that mean? She makes you feel like you are the one that matters which comes naturally because she genuinely cares with a smile. If you are looking for a woman who is attentive, knowledgeable with strengths, passionate, that is driven, a leader but also a team player. You want to be on Team Tameka's team for sure. She is always willing to assist in brainstorming, giving great advice, answering questions, and yes even giving me assignments while leaving me with thought provoking ideas that would lead me down the path of greatness.

Have you ever met someone you can talk to about anything without judgement? How about this? Have you ever had an engaging conversation with an avid listener and awesome communicator that can get you ready for takeoff and you didn't even know you were going anywhere? That's Tameka. I always leave our conversation inspired because her love shines through....Yes, I believe we all have our share of uncertainties, roadblocks, loss, fears but I always remember 2 Timothy 1:7 For God hath not given us the spirit of fear; but of power; and of love, and of a sound mind. She is a living example of a woman that is living it out fearlessly and that encourages me. I am a visual so seeing her growth and her moving strategically has penetrated my soul and mind to encourage me that it's never too late to begin again. Philippians 4:13 states I can do all things through Christ who strengthens me.

Tameka, you have always been a trailblazer, one of a kind, extraordinary and a lovely being so when I think of you and showing love this is what comes to my mind: TAMEKA MCNAIR LOVES by Leading Others Victoriously and Effortlessly.

How has the love I've shown impacted my life in a negative or positive way?

Love transforms. Thank you, Father, because my life has been transformed in many ways for the better. I will take a ride down memory lane and tell you that I haven't forgotten about the countless acts of love you provided to get me through some hills and valleys in my life. Thirsty for God to speak to me while losing a child and a husband in less than two years? Needing direction and you guiding me through God's word and speaking His truth even if that meant I had to go all the way back to my childhood to get to the root of the hurt and anger that I experienced. There is more, how about when we first met, and you asked me at a church conference to be your accountability partner? Guess what? You have been my accountability partner ever since.

We have shared some laughter, tears, joys, disappointments, victories with always giving God the glory and praying to our Father and HE came through. You said Sunshine 'ask God to do the unthinkable' and guess what? HE did. I know that Jesus loves me, this I know for the bible tells me so.... He loved us enough to get us through some hurdles together and that has made a lasting impact. You have been that voice of reason even when at times I was not ready to comply, but I listened, and it helped me tremendously. Life comes with uncertainties daily but it's how you handle them with Gods assurance that HE will see you through. 1 John 4:16 states that God is love and whoever abides in love abides in God, and God abides in him. As I come back from memory lane, did you know, I still recite this statement you shared with me many years ago from another which states, Sunshine "the favor of God is upon you, now wear it like a garment." Wow! I have now changed it to say the favor and love of God is upon me...I shall wear it like a garment. As I arise every morning, I envision while putting on my clothing that I am wearing God's favor and love so I am loved and favored so if I wear it then others will see it! God's love is evident in your life and that same love is contagious. HIS light is shining ever so bright so keep blinding others with his love and know you are loved by Him and others. Tameka continues to be HIS Sunlight.

Based on the definition of love what areas do you feel I have opportunities to grow and where have you seen me excel?

In this verse it defines God's truth and his characteristics of love. It starts off with love is patient and kind, but if I can be brutally honest with you, it is not always easy when others have wronged us whether it be family, friends, significant others, spouses, or enemies. But God! God's love and HIS power is the only thing that can alter our attitudes, grudges and bitterness when it shows up and reveals its ugly head. Transformation is key! I have seen you excel in this area, and I must say I have been mesmerized at your caring response towards those who have hurt you, so I give you a well-deserved thumbs up. There were times I wondered how you could be so loving and kind towards the person that caused you so much pain. The tears you cried, the sleepless nights with a hurting heavy heart and yet still no anger in sight nothing but love beyond the pain.; Tameka you understood this verse in 1 Corinthians 13:4-8 well and for that I commend you for. If there is an opportunity for growth, I would say you have already mastered it in this category. You ask me how? Well, when you show love instead and love still remains even when it's not reciprocated in the manner you desire, that's only God. I saw it in you! The human fleshly side makes that difficult because we are hurt and in pain and carry unforgiveness in our hearts for a minute. Let's stand on truth and do a self-analysis of ourselves because sometimes we love others so much where others may take our kindness and love for granted and not recognize that same love you give out is sometimes not reciprocated. You love hard but that's ok because that's what you do. It hurts but happens, but you keep on loving as God has directed us to do and that is what you did.

Remember Romans 12:14, bless those who persecute you; don't curse them; pray that God will bless them. You are a natural born leader and a person who invest 100 percent into relationships so it's evident you will be looking out for others even when they are not looking out for you or themselves. The relationships that are the Give and Take scenario happens, but it is important to stay guided by God and his living word. He will continually lead you down the right path. We are not perfect, but we are all a work in progress. Envy or boast that's not in your caliber so I can move on. You are indeed a humble woman and definitely not self-seeking therefore you don't keep records of wrong. There are several essentialities listed in this verse, but the overall lesson is God sent his only son to die for us so that's real love. Period.com as you would say. So anytime you get off track go back to this verse and always go back to Jesus your first

Laura's Response

How have I shown you love?

Tameka has shown me love in so many ways from the first day of our friendship, it is hard to pinpoint one instance, but the first day we met definitely stands out.

Usually when I meet people for the first time, they are politely silent while I tic (involuntary movements caused by Tourette's Syndrome) and tolerate my other neurodiverse tendencies like not looking at them directly or rocking back and forth because I cannot sit or stand still. Then they slowly walk away with an excuse to escape from the awkwardness they feel.

The day I met Tameka over four years ago now, we were attending the same women's networking event. I arrived early during the "mingling" time ahead of the main event. Though there were at least 150 people there, I could quickly pick out a handful of women with whom I had met at previous events. I had only been part of this group for a little over a year, so I did not really know anyone that well. I approached a few of the women I knew and engaged in idle chatter, but it was awkward, and I felt out of place as I typically do in these occasions. A small inconvenience. I am aware that as a white cisgender female in a room filled mostly with other white women, I had the privilege of just disappearing into the background until the event started. I could even just hang in the back of a group of women, and "fake listen" to whoever was talking – the privilege of "blending in." Ironically, out of all those women in the hall, only one woman was listening to my heart and intuiting my anxiety, yet I had never even met her before!

As I leaned against the wall like a literal wallflower, praying to disappear, this beautiful woman with a radiant smile comes up to me as if she was reading my mind. Eyes shining, heart open, she says "Hi, I'm Tameka, and these are my friends." She flashes her brilliant, genuine smile, and I immediately smile back and feel an overwhelming wave of joy and relief. This person is so special, I thought to myself. Why would she even go out of her way to say hello to me? Tameka extended love to me that day without having ever met me before. She was the one person in that 150 to show me love and grace – without hesitation. She even offered me a seat next to her and her friends so that I would not sit alone or stand against the back wall. She felt my discomfort, and she gifted me her compassion.

How has the love I've shown impacted your life in a positive or negative way?

I am constantly humbled and forever grateful for Tameka's love and friendship. She has helped me re-learn what it means to restore my self-worth and be kind to myself. I understand now that I cannot truly practice empathy and extend unconditional love to others without loving myself and forgiving myself and others for what may have transpired in my past and is therefore unchangeable but has always weighed heavily on my heart long afterward.

She has taught me how to give and receive grace and love; how to face life's heartbreaks and regrets and learn from them. Tameka's love is truly pure of heart and free of judgment. I feel as if I could talk to her about anything and I could listen and learn from her stories and experiences until the end of time. I am convinced that she has the power to transform lives, not least because she has transformed mine. Tameka makes me feel that our friendship has value to her and that it is cherished, which means so much to me as I hold our friendship dear and precious. She always encourages me to live my values and helps me inch closer to walking in my purpose by modeling it herself to me every day. Unsurprisingly, she is the most mentioned person in my gratitude journal! I feel immensely fortunate to have crossed paths with her and it is an honor to be considered her Friend.

Based on this definition of love, what areas do you feel that I have opportunities to grow and where have you seen me excel?

When I remind myself of unconditional love and what it means, it is easy to think of numerous examples of Tameka excelling in manifesting love in all of the ways described in that definition. From my point of view as her Friend, I would say that Tameka excels at selfless love and patient love. She shows a generosity of unconditional love and kindness that I have never witnessed in a person. Whether you are celebrating an achievement, suffering through a crisis of confidence, or just wanting to connect with your Friend, Tameka's love language shows no preference or bias. She is the sunshine that parts the clouds for me when I am struggling to see the light. She is a patient listener, parsing through my doubts and anxiety and guiding me to clarity and purpose. Her selfless and patient love is an inspiration to me, and she has introduced me to the power of real love and true empathy.

Reading these sentiments from four women in my close circle touched my heart in more ways than one. Their words are affirming and confirm to me that how I'm showing up in the world is true to how I aspire to show up in the world, *by letting love be my Greatest Superpower*.

Chapter Seven: Reflection Exercise

Guiding principles: Love, Patience, Sacrifice, Positivity.

When was the last time that you asked someone to assess how they perceive your love walk? Do you exemplify the attributes of love? Where are your areas of opportunity? Understanding where you currently are with your love walk is your first step to letting love be your Superpower.

Ask 3-4 people who are close to you (explain why they need to be close people) to describe their observation of your love walk using this definition "Love is patient, love is kind, love is long suffering, love is selfless, love is not prideful, love does not envy, love still remains even when it's not reciprocated in the manner that you desire, love does not keep count of any wrongdoings and love never fails is it for eternity".

Ask them to be completely honest as they are supporting you on your journey of letting love be your superpower. Prepare your mind and heart for this activity, leave no room for animosity or defensiveness to set in based on some of the responses you may receive. Some of us may be further along on this journey than others and that is okay. It is not about where you start but where you end. This journey of life is about continuous evolution, taking daily steps to becoming a better version of ourselves.

Ask these three simple questions.

1. How have I shown you love?

2. How has the love I've shown impacted your life in a

positive or negative way?

3. Based on this definition of love, what areas do you feel that I have opportunities to grow and where have you seen me excel? "Love is patient, love is kind, love is long suffering, love is selfless, love is not prideful, love does not envy, love still remains even when it's not reciprocated in the manner that you desire, love does not keep count of any wrongdoings and love never fails it's for eternity."

After reading the letters from your close circle, jot down the list of 5-10 that caused an emotional response in either a good or bad way. Take the next 2-3 weeks to lean into those areas and journal. This may reveal heart-wound areas for you, thrusting you into your journey of healing.

Be kind and patient with yourself, as this journey will enable you to avoid cutting others with your broken pieces.

In closing, I hope that this book has inspired, encouraged and empowered you to look at the moments of uncertainty in a different way as well as owning your' narrative (story) without shame. No matter what type of experience we have or what challenges we go through, we can choose to find a positive perspective.

Homing in on the silver-lining ("something good that can be found in a bad situation") and only speaking words of positivity over your situation. Sometimes we underestimate the power associated with the words that we speak. Choosing to focus on the positive perspective sets you free from the agony of the experience. It does not change the experience itself, and it is okay to feel sad, angry, or scared. But it provides a way to get you through it, and I would even attest that it aids you in your healing process. We have so many things to be grateful for—I challenge you to find moments in every experience to celebrate.

Do not concede too soon in moments of uncertainty, as your Victory awaits you.

Own your own destiny, Stick to your dreams and passions, Thrive in the space you are in now.

CLOSING THOUGHTS

This book is dedicated to anyone who has experienced Uncertainty in their life which caused them to question their worth, jeopardized their peace or caused them to become immobilized by fear. If we don't concede in those moments, we will find that tenacity and perseverance is built within us. 'You' are stronger than what you think and you being *Victorious* is bigger than you! You are someone else's *Hope* and *Inspiration* in their moments of uncertainty.

Know that as long as we're on this journey called 'life' there will always be moments of uncertainty that we will encounter. The key is anchoring to those specks of positivity that can carry you through those scary, devastating, and sometimes immobilizing moments of uncertainty.

ABOUT THE AUTHOR

Tameka McNair holds an undergraduate degree in Industrial Engineering with a focus in Human Factors and an MBA with a focus in Leadership. Currently, Tameka is a Director at Microsoft driving digital employee experience success. Her personal mission is to Empower everyone that she encounters to become the best version of themselves and to discover their purpose - encouraging others to reach for the stars and to not stop until they obtain them all!

Her unique style, personality, and commitment to walking in her authentic truth has played a major part in navigating her life and career. Inspired by her experience overcoming a wide range of obstacles, Tameka seeks to encourage others to pursue their dreams despite the various challenges they may face. Tameka is a long-time advocate of DEI (Diversity, Equity, & Inclusion) and has helped establish employee resource groups to push DEI initiatives. She is an active mentor to both adults and youth in underserved communities and passionate about encouraging youth and minorities to explore STEM careers. She is also the cofounder of the Women IN Energy Conference.

Within the last 10 years, Tameka has made four industry switches (Manufacturing, Energy, Software and Retail), each leveraging her technical expertise, desire to solve challenging problems, customer obsession and ability to navigate across various disciplines. Tameka aspires to become the CEO of a Fortune 100 company.

Made in the USA
Middletown, DE
23 April 2023

29219354R00071